PRAISE FOR CINELLE BARNES

"A gifted writer with a compelling story about her life in the Philippines."

—*Kirkus Reviews*

"Barnes's story is unforgettable, and highly relevant to 2019 America."

—*Publishers Weekly*

"We are all immigrants in constant quest for freedom. Cinelle Barnes, Filipino American author, inspires with her endurance. But, like all stories, freedom is merely the beginning. For Barnes, life continues. This time, Barnes is ready. Her freedom empowers her."

—*Positively Filipino*

"Cinelle Barnes considers how the chaos and discipline of dance kept the disparate parts of her being stitched together."

—*Longreads*

"With compassion and conviction, Barnes bears witness to stories that so often go untold—and asserts the possibility of a world where those we love have the freedom to tell their own."

—Zeyn Joukhadar, author of *The Map of Salt and Stars*

"Cinelle Barnes's essays explore what it means to live authentically as a woman, a person of color, an immigrant, a human being, not in the hands or eyes of others but in her own heart. Barnes tells her story with clarity and honesty and, in doing so, clears a path for the rest of us to follow."

—Victoria Loustalot, author of *Future Perfect: A Skeptic's Search for an Honest Mystic*, *Living Like Audrey: Life Lessons from the Fairest Lady of All*, and *This Is How You Say Goodbye: A Daughter's Memoir*

"Barnes's deft writing crosses gaps in time, understanding, and experience, illuminating important truths about our country and culture while also allowing us to bear witness to her own fight for healing, justice, and belonging. . . . Cinelle Barnes is a writer to treasure."

—Nicole Chung, author of *All You Can Ever Know*

A WAY HOME

OTHER TITLES BY CINELLE BARNES

Monsoon Mansion

Malaya: Essays on Freedom

A Measure of Belonging: Twenty-One Writers of Color on the New American South

A WAY HOME

A MEMOIR OF LOSING YOURSELF AND THE BEAUTY OF RETURNING

CINELLE BARNES

Published by Little A, New York
www.apub.com

EU product safety contact:
Amazon Media EU S. à r.l.
38, avenue John F. Kennedy, L-1855 Luxembourg
amazonpublishing-gpsr@amazon.com

ISBN-13: 9781662510618 (hardcover)
ISBN-13: 9781662510625 (paperback)
ISBN-13: 9781662510601 (digital)

Cover design by Emily Mahon

Cover image: © Kwangmoozaa, © Lotus Images / Shutterstock; © VectorUp, © Nora Carol Photography, © guytoon / Getty

Printed in the United States of America

First edition

For myself
and for everyone
who helped her find the way home

We shall not cease from exploration
And the end of all our exploring
Will be to arrive where we started
And know the place for the first time

—T. S. Eliot, from "Little Gidding"

Contents

Given the intensity of a few sections, I offer content warnings to help readers prepare. This book contains descriptions of childhood neglect, financial abuse by a parent, and medical trauma (detailed brain surgery and temporary loss of cognitive abilities and bodily control). No depictions are gratuitous, but they might be intense enough that some readers might benefit from advance notice.

A Note from the Author

Dear reader:

I'm so grateful that you and I are here.

On November 14, 2023, I suffered a traumatic brain injury while sitting in a café in Charleston, enjoying my coffee with oat milk like it was any other day. But then my world turned upside down. In an article I wrote for *Travel + Leisure* in February 2025, "Let It Wash Over You," I described it as such:

Something clapped in my head, and before I could place my hand where I felt the thunder, the floor and walls were above me. Everything was in orbit: the charger, the pen, my coffee, and laptop. The sun burned my eyes, and suddenly even the blue light of my phone and computer were unbearably bright. I tried to turn away, but my neck was locked in place. I closed my eyes. Feeling around for my phone, muscle memory allowed me to text my husband an SOS.

I was writing the first draft of this article the same month I was supposed to be finishing this book, a travelogue about my return to the Philippines after a twenty-year separation. That was never an easy story to tell, and now I was attempting to piece it together while also trying to remember the names of my husband, Stephen, and our daughter, Anouk. At the hospital, I had to practice spelling my name like a kindergartner, and I was quizzed on details that suddenly didn't come to me automatically, like my home address. It would have been easier to give up on writing both the article and the book, or on writing altogether. Or on recovering my whole person.

But the fateful reporting trip to coastal Mississippi for *Travel + Leisure*, the last one I took with my short-term memory intact, had given me a glimpse of the resilience of the communities who are still rebuilding post-Katrina. As I wrote, the people I met there taught me that to be creative is to hope.

After my arrival at the emergency room, Stephen would be told I'd had a brain aneurysm rupture. I had mere hours to get lifesaving brain surgery, and the doctors said the procedure would come at a cost: I could lose some abilities, including writing and my mobility. I would spend the next weeks in the hospital, recovering from both the cranial hemorrhage and the operation, fighting off overwhelming pain and complications, and entertaining the doctors with my quirky answers to their questions (*Can you tell us who you are?* I'm a writer who makes friends on travels).

With a traumatic brain injury like the one I survived, many people experience both their inner and outer worlds quite differently than they did before. Changes to the brain can affect a person's memory, attention, concentration, problem-solving and multitasking abilities; speech and word recall; and reasoning skills. These changes can alter the way a person makes sense of, or engages with, the world around them, and thus up to nearly 70 percent of people who sustain a head injury may experience depersonalization (an altered perception of self) and/or derealization (a sustained feeling of surrealness and an alteration in one's perception of the environment and of time).

I experienced such changes in the year following my brain aneurysm rupture, during which time I relied on audio recordings, medical records, my journals, calendars, sketchbooks, photographs, and videos—not to mention so much help from family, friends, editors, my literary agent, and volunteer typists and dictation apps—to complete this book. I hope that in your reading you feel not only my strength but also the collective spirit that brought this book forth. I hope you feel not only the heart behind my words but also the many beating hearts that supported me and afforded me time, space, and capacity to complete this work.

When you find yourself in the breaths or breaks between the chapters about my journey home to the Philippines and the moments I've captured from my brain injury recovery, I hope you feel the weight and embrace of community, of mutual aid, and of what it means to be an "independent" artist, which I think is mostly an experience of community and shared pursuits. The way home is rebellious in this sense: It is rebellious to the "bootstrap" mentality many tout and to solitary, individualistic, and rather fatal, nihilistic ways that the American Dream exploitatively, sadistically "rewards." I'm so glad to have been born Filipino, which is to say I was destined for togetherness.

Throughout this memoir, you'll hear echoes of this and of a phrase my daughter coined when she was only eight years old: *We have a good team.* As it was, and is, for me, I hope this message is fortifying for you.

My other wish is that reading this book expands your understanding of a memoir from a mere retelling of what happens to an individual to a capturing of how an individual affects the world. (And I hope you consider what this means in the age of AI.) Sometimes, our individual effect on the world is but a quiet endeavor. This book is quieter than my other books. It's been years since I first embarked on this project and then found myself incapacitated by a neurological condition. Later still, I found myself and my family in the chaos of current political events and movements, so I understand now that this quiet is exactly where the pulse of this book is. This quiet is exactly what I was in pursuit of all the years I was an undocumented immigrant, whether I knew it then or not. This quiet is what I worked to give myself because it was exactly what the United States refused, and refuses, to give me.

There is so much peace in these pages, dear reader, and it is that peace they absolutely want none of us on the right side of history to have. The pulse of this book is my stead: how I stayed in this country for as long as I did so that I could legally return to my motherland and then safely return to the home I'd built (and am now rebuilding) with my husband and daughter in coastal Carolina. It is about how I stayed alive and continued into my living after a brain aneurysm rupture and emergency brain surgery and how much of that living is the writing itself. At every read and phase of this book, I was reminded that just because something is quiet doesn't mean it is benign. Of course, there is a parallel here: My neurosurgeons believe that the aneurysm was congenital, there in my skull since before birth, so seismic and yet silent, erupting thirty-eight years later without warning.

Meanwhile, the quiet I painted here as images of my home, family, friendships, vocations, and locations is hopefully what you take away from this work that, because of a major health event and a brush with death, almost didn't reach completion. They say the best fiction mirrors life so closely, it is believable. And they say the best nonfiction is so incredible, as in unbelievable and extraordinarily true. This quiet is then explosive in these terms: An ordinary life is miraculous, given what I've been through and given the perilous and inhumane sanctions, the limitations, and the systemic burdens placed upon immigrants like me by the powers that be.

Some background on my immigration journey: Deposited to San Francisco's arrivals terminal by the automatic shuffling that people do at airports, my sixteen-year-old self waited in the cold and fog that March 2003 morning, underdressed for the Bay Area weather and unprepared in every sense for my unexpected adoption. I was told by my oldest half sister, who until then was my guardian, that I was coming to America to find and visit relatives, and this was exactly the reason for visiting I declared at immigration. I didn't yet know, standing there with one duffel bag and a beat-up but respectable pair of white Tretorn sneakers, that I had been shuffled into a kind of hostage situation: no way to legally stay for a chance at life in the US and yet no way to survive as an orphaned teen in the Philippines. I would be legally adopted in 2004, but I would already be too old to receive naturalization benefits as an adoptee at the age of seventeen. I became undocumented.

I wouldn't see, for two decades, the place of my birth, where I had helped to plan prom and for which I played in the U-17 women's soccer team. (The latter two details surprise Americans the most when I tell them of my life back then. It comes as a shock, somehow, that my old life was a full life. And after the traumatic brain injury, I've had to work to accept this too: that my old life was indeed brimming, and although I now live with cognitive deficits and life adaptations and fluctuating daily rhythms, I can assume a full life for me and my family still.)

In this book, I talk a whole lot about fate, destiny, kismet—whatever you want to call it. Writing this note to you in 2025 makes me laugh a little. Over the course of two decades, much has changed for me and much has remained the same. Some things, more bad than good, have intensified. I write this to you from a sweaty South Carolina afternoon steeping not only in 60 percent humidity but also the stifling political climate of late. I am an immigrant woman who was once an immigrant girl. Danger has followed me for most of my days. I hope you see now why I wrote a travelogue: because it felt frivolous, careless. For a short window of time (less than three years) I could travel freely, easily, safely. A voice in my head told me to not only go but also write. To preserve. To remember. It was a post-9/11 luxury.

See, after 9/11, legislation signed by George W. Bush would result in the formation of the Transportation Security Administration, the required screening of all checked bags, and the appointment of more federal air marshals on flights. It also set into motion changes within immigration and family court, forever altering not just how we travel but the to-and-fro of families, or would-be families. It wouldn't be the first time the law encroached on family life, but it would be a turning point. My life became a tug between mobility and immobility in that I did not have the credentials to safely cross national borders or to easily traverse city or county or state limits, but I also had to stay on the go, on the move, anxious feet forever on a fictitious accelerator. (Today, this might remind you of video clips you've seen on your social media feed or news sources. Again, I'm here to preserve, to help us all remember.) Fed a scarcity mindset and an all-American fear of lagging behind, of getting caught, and of not being good enough so as not to be further disvalued in a country where a human's worth netted according to their usefulness and their ability to activate and monetize such, there was no rest. When it became en vogue to practice "self-care," I didn't quite know what that meant. I didn't know how to apply the virtue of rest when rest in itself was a mode, an object—yet another desirable product at a price, a thing to not just long for but strive for, a number following any number of decimal points and zeros, branded material for aspirational cost. From

2020 to 2023, in some intended ironic sense, I meant to give you some "light reading." And I meant to show myself (and other immigrants) something out of the ordinary—again a play on words: how to travel light.

Also extraordinary: I live. At least half of aneurysm ruptures lead to death within twenty-four hours of the onset of hemorrhage, and an overwhelming number of survivors, mostly women, wake up from brain surgery with severe cognitive disabilities and partial or total paralysis. Please know that I've achieved all that I set out to do, which is to finish this work and honor who I was and who I am becoming. When it was my time to leave, I set out to many places. When it was my fate to stay, I did. I hope my memoir inspires you to listen attentively to which of the two a moment calls you to do. After all, it is the only way home.

Again, I'm so thankful that you and I are here, alive *and* living.

Cinelle Barnes
August 2025

PART I

FIRST POINT OF DEPARTURE
Charleston, South Carolina
Unceded Edisto Natchez-Kusso Land

Where I started and raised a family,
And weathered the pandemic,
And confronted a long-lost idea.

—May 2020–April 2021

Dispatches from Recovery

2023

I'm woken up by screams for help. A man's voice, an older one. He's begging for someone to get him out of his bed. He's asking why he's in a gown, like I'm in a gown. Why the tubes in his arms? Why the bandages? He keeps yelling, always ending with a question mark, as if he's calling out from the dark. The rush of feet throbs through the wall parting us. I hear them mumbling, hushing him down, shushing him—shush, shush, shush. He's just had brain surgery, they say. They ask him for his name, and all he says is "WHAT? WHAT?" *They repeat the words he can't grasp.* Brain surgery. Hospital. *He is—we are—on the ninth floor, the neuro floor. Shush-shush. He says again,* "WHAT? WHAT?" *They repeat, repeat, repeat. He cries. A woman's voice, soft like pink, floats above the noise. She says, "It's okay, honey. It's okay." And just when I think the panic has died down, he screams again,* "WHAT?" *Then, like a wounded wolf,* "WHO?"

In my room, this beige-and-white one I've woken in, a whimper unfurls like my consciousness, like an infant's hand. It's the whimper of a child. A girl. I turn my eyes to where she sits on the bed: at my feet. She looks to the wall from where the panic next door pours through, like a watcher trembling on the outskirts of a forest fire. Her shoulders rise sharp and rise again, and this is how I know. She's scared, this girl. And somehow I feel the need to comfort her. My mouth dry, I say, because I still have my words, "It's okay. He's just confused. They're helping him."

She turns to me, eyes close together and tired, a quiver in her lip, and says, "Why is he screaming?"

I say, "I think"—because I can still think—"he doesn't know who or where he is."

"That can happen?" she asks and cups her hands over her ears. I see now that I haven't comforted her. I blink, slow so I can reach for more words. I reach for the color pink, for its softness. I make it my voice. I say, sweetly so she won't know I'm in pain, "It's okay. I know where I am. I know who I am. And I know who you are."

Her hands fall from her ears to my feet, and I feel my toes thaw. She says, her face open, "You do, Mama? You know?"

I know and I don't.

I know my name and hers and his. I know the four-digit code to unlock the phone on the hospital tray. I know which hospital this is and where it is in relation to the ranch-style house the three of us call home. I know I have a cat and that he eats his dinner every evening at five. When the nurses ask if I know why I'm here, I know what to say: I had a brain aneurysm. When the tall doctor with the bouncy brown hair walks in, I know his name: Dr. Hubbard.

I know his name because before my eyes closed on the operating table, he said, "Hello, I'm Dr. Hubbard, and I'm one of the neurosurgery residents here." I also know his name because once everything was set in place, once the bleeding had been stopped and I opened my eyes again, he said, "Hello, me again, Dr. Hubbard. You did good. How do you feel?" I didn't know what time or day it was, but I knew the pain in my stomach was separate from the pain in my head, so to Dr. Hubbard I responded, "I feel . . . like eating fried chicken. Can someone get me fried chicken?" At this he laughed and patted my shoulder and said that I will do great. And I didn't know when "will" would happen and what "great" meant or entailed.

Now he's introducing himself to the tall white man I call Stephen, who seems even taller now, and when they shake hands, I don't feel like I'm a part of it, in the way a child might feel when her parents and pediatrician are talking about the rash that is nothing to worry about, nothing to worry about, and yet the child feels like there's a creature taking root in her palm.

Dr. Hubbard presses a button to incline my bed so I can see the monitor better. A few clicks and there appear gray swirls and gray spaces, gray tangles and gray loops. This, the all of it, he says, is my brain.

Where the picture is mostly space, a loop curls up and around to meet the darkest of grays—and here Dr. Hubbard presses his finger. "Glue," he says, "to stop the bleeding." Like a cork, *I think to myself. Then he says, pointing at the nothing, the all of it, "We had to sacrifice this area," and the word* sacrifice *makes me look harder at all the emptiness, all that the blood was hungry for, all it had consumed, and I feel the need to say* WHAT? WHAT?, *like the man next door. And because I detect the fear in me, I assume there is fear in her, and I say,* "STOP," *to the kind-but-too-fast Dr. Hubbard.*

When he stops, I scan the room to find her, and there she is by the window that gives us the only light that doesn't hurt—sunlight—and when I ask, "Does this scare you?" she shakes her head and darts her eyes to the monitor. I look where she's looking, hoping to see there's nothing to worry about, nothing to worry about.

1

Escape Reality

May 2020

I'm sitting on our living room rug, fatigued from the quadruple pandemic burdens on women: childcare, home care, culture care, and work. And then: The toilet in the main bathroom gurgles.

I hear the bubbling sound and rush to it, calling for Stephen to abandon his movie as I dash past him, my voice equally loud and interfering like a passing siren. When I step foot on the cold tile, the tub has filled a quarter of the way with brown wastewater. The toilet is about to overflow. I cry for help louder. Stephen comes to the bathroom with our pandemic pet bunny in his hands. At the sight, he gags. He scrambles to the smaller en suite where we keep the bunny's pen. Before he can return our pet to its enclosure, the same brown water bubbles out of that bathroom's drain and toilet too, making plastic boats out of the bunny's toys.

We both call to Anouk, "Towels! Quick!"

She scurries to the linen closet and then to each of us, arms around the nice towels we got for our wedding.

I say, "Not those! The scrappy ones!"

She throws them at my feet anyway, knowing that her mother is crazy for wanting to save the nice towels when the water is coming up toward the threshold. She takes the bunny from her dad and pivots, stomping toward the living room, where she will build a couch-cushion enclosure for her furry friend. Stephen calls a plumber. It rings, no answer. Now on speaker, he tries again before dialing another number.

We have afforded very recently, through my myriad freelance gigs and NGO contracting job and Stephen's middle school teacher salary and substitute teaching and sports camp coaching, a down payment for a ranch-style house on a quiet bend. A coveted Charleston house on Zillow, my offer for it won not because I was the highest bidder but, according to the sellers, the kindest. They felt grace and good intentions from me at the open house, they told my real estate agent, felt them so strongly that they turned down an earlier offer for $17,000 more than what I could give. I have at least that: my unmistakably Filipino kindheartedness.

It's what I've built our home on, this softness. In two months' time, I filled this home with soft things I daisy-stitched, hemmed, laundered, sun-bleached, buttoned and unbuttoned, and sniffed and succumbed to for their sweet baby smell. It's square footage I've furnished according to where the sun hits on certain times of the day and based on my and my daughter's preferred Baby Spice color scheme, making a strategically angled armchair or sofa feel like, when you're lying on it, a luxury resort palapa. I'm quite proud of myself. With handed-down IKEA recliners, my mother-in-law's heirloom dressers and her unwanted mattresses ("too soft"), and my Hello Kitty fabrics, I've turned our first house into a would-be Four Seasons x Sanrio collaboration. It's all about textures, angles. Lines. It's all about tricking the mind.

It's what I believed the news and intel I have through my NGO job told me to do: cushion myself and my loved ones from words that are suddenly ubiquitous: "unprecedented times."

We wait for someone to pick up the phone as we throw more of whatever fabrics we can find onto the bathroom floors, creating dams to halt the flood. Beloved and thinning T-shirts, Hello Kitty pillowcases, the felted blanket we always fall asleep under when on the couch: They're all steeped like tea bags now. My stomach twists as I scoop embroidered washcloths and loofahs from the wastewater rising in the tub.

My soft things: ruined. The bathrooms having erupted, the entire house smells like a train station bathroom at six o'clock in the morning. My stomach keeps twisting. I'm nauseous from an earlier back-and-forth with family and the back-and-forth about everything in my mind and from the thought of something foreign, something toxic, penetrating the home I've created.

We wait for salvation by way of a Roto-Rooter plumber. Stephen says, pushing back an inch-tall wall of water with a rolled-up bedsheet, "Is this like the water you write about all day?"

I nod. While so many of my friends and family members have been laid off due to the ripple effects of the pandemic, my NGO colleagues and I work without sleep, without breaks, without all the funds needed to fight a global health crisis. Some of our staff in Haiti, all considered essential workers, have been held at gunpoint by gangs for boxes of supplies en route to a rural village where orphans have gone for days without food or drink. Other coworkers in Uganda and Tanzania brace themselves for the coronavirus coming for the overcrowded refugee camps and settlements where they operate. They dispatch these stories to me electronically. And I read or listen to the dispatches from my kitchen island, which is now both an office and a classroom, protected from the outside forces that my colleagues have to work and live through.

Stephen shakes his head and says, his whiteness and Southernness coming through, "Gol-ly," to the kind of work I've taken on since bowing out of literary publishing and pretending that it's wise (the paycheck, the health insurance)—noble, even—to sign up for a nine-to-five in the humanitarian sector, the "good" sector, the sector that supposedly remedies whatever there is to remedy in nations recovering from colonialism . . . like my home country.

Toxic water filled with industrial, animal, and human waste; the extreme lack of water in one region; the extreme overabundance in another part of the world: the very topics that have shaped my prose, if you can call it that, since I said ta-ta to book writing. Today, we're surrounded with sickness: the coronavirus going around in my family and in the world and all the waterborne diseases swimming and multiplying and mutating in our water. And every day for the past two years now I have been surrounded by a nagging regret for having left my first love, literature. For money, for stability, for this house now reeking of sewage, I abandoned some dreams and felt my way in the dark toward new ones. The immigrant mother in me said, "You're certainly not the first to do this. You're certainly not the first to reinvent."

"Yep, hello?" the plumber says on speaker. We hear his keys jingle.

Stephen answers, describing the situation too politely and too specifically and too verbosely (too *Southernly*). There is no urgency in his delivery. I roll my eyes at him as if to say, *This is not your college admissions essay.* But he continues as is, so I talk over him, pleading that the plumber come soon.

The first instruction the plumber gives, as he gets off the phone, is to not touch the water. He says, as his website says, "This water is contaminated and dangerous."

"Tanginang madre de Dios," I say, as I've caught myself saying sporadically since lockdown began.

Stephen smirks, lips tight and quivery, trapping an oncoming and ill-timed linguistics joke in his mouth.

The plumber arrives, and he's concerned like a fireman is concerned and quick like a fireman is quick. He can't be older than us. He talks without looking us in the eye, always moving, always sucking air through his teeth before retrieving another tool from his truck. Every time I hear the sucking sound, I think, *Learn, girl, learn. This is how you protect your home next time.*

His white truck color-blocks against the dark of night, the popped trunk catching moonlight and giving gifts made of metal and made for rescuing clueless homeowning kids like us. It's true; we're just kids. We cup our hands over our mouths or clasp them in prayer at our chests. Deliverance has come. Salvation is seeing someone your age act like they know what they're doing so you can follow along. The plumber, this savior, runs a snake through our sewage line, meters and meters deep, slithering and slinking it through and around the circuit of whatnot under our house (also known as our savings, our capital, our only asset in a country concerned with all that appreciates, or what I was taught, as an immigrant child, was the zenith of my existence here). When it seems like he's hit it, whatever it is, he gives the snake a little jig and then a big shake, and clears the clog. He flushes out the nastiness that has invaded our home and threatened our health, safety, and sense of peace, out to the municipal line. Our life is back to normal—our clumsy, clueless normal. As Stephen signs forms and hands over a credit card to accrue more debt, I return to the living room, where Anouk's dancing to a tune from the new *Trolls* soundtrack. She waves me over; she knows I know the song.

She says, as the playlist loads the next dance hit, "It'll all be okay, Mama. We'll be okay, just like the refugees you write about will be okay and our family in New York will be okay and the world will be okay. We have a good team."

I don't know what she means by such words: *okay, we, good, team.* I pretend to believe her, like I've pretended to believe in safety in a house, peace from an office job, and the rewards of bootstrappin' and good, honest, head-down immigrant work. I sell this belief with my vibrato. I sing like she sings, loud and proud and terribly off-key, like on the other side of uncertainty is someone listening, craning their neck to hear better, to bring their ear closer to this hope that her continued innocence has to offer. The bunny hops around in the square of cushions that somehow haven't collapsed on him, even with our dancing and jumping. The little guy is padded and protected from our glass-shattering voices and from our off-beat feet and from the water that nearly drowned and poisoned him, and I think, *This is her doing.* She conjures possibility with her locomotor, fine-motor, and critical-thinking skills, along with her faith, not in some higher power but in our lowly, earthly, flawed mechanics called, on this side of Earth, kin, and on the side of it where I once lost baby hairs and baby teeth, kapwa. I'll hold on to that Filipino sense of shared inner self, at least for now, when I can't seem to hold on to the reality or feeling of softness I've long tried to conjure. I'll believe her like I believe the wisdom and knowledge and dollar estimates of the plumber. Maybe she has answers. Maybe she has questions I don't yet know to ask.

Dispatches from Recovery

2023

Where did I go when my eyes closed?

The man I call Stephen returns every morning after he drops her off at school. Every day I wait for my second nap so I can awake from it with her next to me, smelling like a classroom and watching a video on the phone that unlocks with my face or the four digits I somehow know.

Every day he brings bags of soft things. A plushie. Clean underwear. A felted throw and slippers that fit my feet. Felt-tip markers and a sketch pad to help me pass the time. Cards people have sent from all over. "I brought your things," he says while laying them down on the hospital tray with such care, almost making up for the way the night nurse pricks my hands and arms every hour, every night. But this Stephen, he is gentle and kind. And I believe I am kind too. "My things," I say, smiling and reaching for them as far as I can, which isn't at all far, but I do it to mirror his kindness.

Today he has a mason jar of flowers he cut from the yard, periwinkle pom-poms begging to be touched. He says, bringing them close to my hand, "Can you believe you grew these?"

The truth is I don't know what to believe. I have all these memories in a bank in my head. Images, voices. Today I woke up from my first nap wondering how they made it there—to the gray loops and spaces. I don't know if I own them, or I'm just safekeeping them, or if they're mine for the moment but not for too long, or if I dreamt them. Or if I'm still dreaming. Or if the gray loops and spaces are in my skull at all, or if they're still in Dr. Hubbard's monitor. Or if I'm the monitor, a machine pushed around. Or if I close my eyes long and hard enough, I'll find out that I am just someone's placeholder.

Too many questions—they tire me. Too many thoughts for which I must reach the words. Reach, reach. When my eyes close, I might be taking a nap. And when my eyes close, I am most certainly reaching, reaching, stretching far for where I've gone.

2

Domestic

May 2020

"When can we go to the Philippines?" Anouk asks again from the tub.

She's been asking nonstop for weeks.

The first time this came up, we were also in water. At my wit's end only a month into quarantine, I'd purchased an inflatable pool that we filled with water from our garden spout. I'd forgotten to order a hose for the spout, so we'd collected the water ice-cream container by ice-cream container, and carried it to the source, our oasis on this near-ninety-degree, climate-catastrophic day. I remember thinking that the task—multiplied by the length of time and the distance on foot—resembled the part of my childhood in the Philippines spent walking to a poso, or a groundwater pump.

"It's not so bad," Anouk says as she plops down into the three inches of pitter-patter water. I want to tell her that our little activity is nothing like what I had to do growing up, but instead I say, "Aren't you glad we have a pool in quar—"

She splashes me. She does it before she hears what she knows is coming next: another one of those aren't-you-grateful-fors.

"Splash me back, Mom!"

I splash her back using the lid of an ice-cream container. I get her so good, she's both delighted and mad. Our game turns into a tussle. She's now big enough (or maybe the pandemic has just aged me) that if she pounces on me, my elbows or knees give a little. I fall back into the water. Sitting back up, wishful thinking rises to the air with me.

"Hey, when the world opens up again," I tell her, apocalyptic language now so everyday, "we should go somewhere fun, don't you think?"

"Like the Philippines!" She splashes me again.

"No, not there. Why there?" I wonder who taught her this. I want to slap them. I have not been to the country of my birth since I was sixteen years old, in the spring of 2003, before there were even websites like Facebook or devices like iPhones. Before I was adopted by an American family the following fall, the adoption process just taking a tad too long for Immigration Court (I'd turned seventeen, too old to become a citizen through adoption). Before my adoptive mother bought me my first puff jacket for my first full winter, and I started living as an undocumented person, unable to travel into and out of the United States.

I grew up on the outskirts of Manila, nearly nine thousand miles from where I am today, doing what a lot of mothers do at the end of the day. I am giving my child a bath, readying her for bedtime so that Stephen and I can watch exactly fourteen minutes of television before we fall asleep, legs crisscrossed under a felted blanket on the couch with the cushions I paid extra for because they have just the right hold for my bad lower back and just the right give for Anouk's achy, unstable hips. I am sixteen hours away by plane from the city where my own mother never gave me a bath. I encompass motherhood, a marriage, a hodgepodge writing career, two university degrees, a religion or lack thereof, and an adolescence of unraveling away from the colorful, labyrinthine streets, the heckling vendors, and the honking jeepneys of what, to this day, I consider one of the most vibrant cities ever created by man.

It's like an ancient civilization to me: hidden under the rubble of what it took to get to my now-life, holding history and myth. It is a city I don't much speak of on the rare occasion that I do speak to my daughter of where I am from. Where I am from, how I've fabricated it: a general vicinity in the Pacific, a long word she knows, as in *ark-ee-pehl-ah-go*, somewhere north of Indonesia and south of Taiwan, a lateral neighbor of Cambodia and Vietnam. It is where coconut trees grow and sway, like she has seen in her favorite *Moana*. It's a group of more than seven thousand sun-kissed islands we Filipinos call, as in our national anthem, land of the morning.

It's not only a place that is oceans away. It's a world away. We would have to cross portals, shift paradigms, shape-shift. At least I would need to shape-shift back. But I'm not the teenage girl who was ripped from her home by a surprise international adoption. I'm no longer the varsity soccer team captain who was relinquished to family court by a mother and a father facing separate but equally exigent criminal cases. I am one overseas-crossing; three interstate migrations; one Southern dialect; many pat-downs and fingerprintings; several asylum and immigrant petition rejections; countless harassments gone unreported for fear of deportation; tens of thousands of dollars paid to lawyers and to federal institutions and to that scumbag in "legal services" infomercials on the Filipino Channel; *twenty solid years*; and a new, young, hip, happy little family and happy little home away from—it hurts to say it—home.

"When can we go to the Philippines?"

I look at the daughter to whom I've sold the concept of endless domestic (but really, Southeastern) travel as a decoy for the international trips I can't afford, couldn't legally make happen until just two years ago, in 2018, didn't have the right passport for much of my life in the United States, and now cannot participate in because the world is on lockdown. I always knew this question would come up, but at what frequency—and with what gravity or, worse, with what amount of playfulness and cuteness—it would arrive, I had not anticipated. I believed for a time that with enough diversions, we would dodge the question.

"Mama, when, when?"

I have given countless hours to freelance and salaried work in exchange for hours together on domestic flights and road trips, staying at La Quintas and Airbnbs, eating at subpar breakfast buffets, even on weekends when I'd rather stay in and quietly recuperate from the inhumane demands of my combined freelance and NGO jobs. For some familial sense of well-traveledness: I get up and I sweat and I cry, or as the world I'm in likes to say, I hustle—like an American millennial.

These spurts of domestic travel—to Asheville, Atlanta, Charlotte, Orlando, Savannah, St. Augustine, and the occasional JetBlue to New York—are nothing but distractions from the one truly longed for (by her, by me, even by her dad) yet unspoken-of trip that would cost too much (at least $1,000 one-way, per person), take too long (at least sixteen hours nonstop), and require plenty of labor of the logistic, mental, emotional, physical, and possibly metaphysical kinds.

Later, in the tub in the house in the city in which I had to display my kindness to win at modern real estate games, she is wondering not if but when I would take her to the Philippines. How bold and assuming. In other words: innocent. This is the way of children: You've just bought them a house, and they ask for a yogurt; you've reached your overtime quota so you could fill their memory bank with Disney World and Broadway experiences, and they want to see, not instead of but as well as, the place and people that gave you that high-pitched laugh and that not-classically trained but impeccable chef's palate.

She was born this way. I know this, and others have repeatedly told me: She's so curious and so good and deserves the world. She was also born in the water—pushed into a birthing pool and introduced to the outside world without much shock, swimmingly transferring from one aqueous environment to another. Water is the abundance she knows. She was swimming assisted at five months old and on her own before she was in school. It is water, or bilateral movement in it, that's helped align the uneven hips she was born with. It's what's consistently relieved her physical pain. Water: doctor's orders. Also water: where we are both from. Why wouldn't she want to be in—as I've both proudly and reluctantly said—the most pristine, maybe even healing, waters in the world?

Preternaturally adept, our neighbor Kathleen, a retired pediatric nurse, used to pipe as she and her dogs walked past us, eyes narrowed at me under her reflective Oakleys: "Promise me, give her the world." Women like her, they love to mind us in public. They yap to tell us how cute we are, how tan we are, how preternaturally adept our children are.

Oh, Kathleen, I always wanted to say, *but what if the world was never mine to give?* What if I'd been restricted by the government and my finances from doing a semester in Florence as a college student, or backpacking through Costa Rica as a fresh grad, or wintering in Cancún in celebration of my small but meaningful publishing successes? How, then, do I flash a boarding pass and say, "This here, this small but meaningful seat, is mine"?

Anouk no longer needs scooping up from the tub, but I still do it. I get down on my knees and reach forward, folding her into a towel as I swing her onto the bath mat, my knees cracking like walnuts despite my efforts to look strong. She hears the sound of my near-middle age against the floor tiles, chuckles, then kisses me on the forehead for some kind of consolation. "One day," she says, "you won't be able to do this, and I'll take care of you."

"Sure will, girl," I tell her and kiss her back on her wet forehead. "You sure will."

Dispatches from Recovery

Late 2023

There are more questions:

"Can you tell us who you are?" (I can answer this, no problem, but there lies a gap between who I say I am and who I feel I am, and I'm afraid that if I'm not careful, into the distance I'll fall.)

"Can you tell us why you're here?" (The nurses divert their eyes when they ask this, perhaps because they know that "WHAT-WHAT" *and "Yes, I had a brain aneurysm" are two faces of the same pain.)*

"Can you tell us what that is?" (They almost always point at the clock on the wall, so obsessed with time. I want to roll my eyes, but I never do. But there is, thank my luck, Sammy, a young nurse technician with a raspy voice made for Old Hollywood, who instead asks me what it is I've drawn in my sketchbook. And these are the moments when I feel I am here, really here, able to talk about something I know I made.)

"Can you tell us who they are?" (They mean Stephen and Anouk, and I am able to say just so. I can name their favorite foods and colors, and I know their birthdays and most-played songs. What I don't know is if they know that I don't know if I'm the right version of the person they love or if they're the incorrect version of the people I fought death for, or if I am in the wrong universe, or if I'm two seconds too late or two seconds too soon.)

3

Mother Tongue

I have an otherworld.

I wake up speaking in the languages of this realm. "Umaga na," I say as I roll over to kiss Stephen awake. I say it at daybreak, the sweetness of my mother tongue lolling out of my slightly parted lips, leaching out and rescinding like sweet baby drool. I don't yet know this, but it's a symptom of long COVID (which I contracted in November) that I don't completely exit dream-sense each morning, sporadically speaking throughout the day in Tagalog, my home country's national language and my home region's dialect. I don't make sense of it until he asks what it means.

"What *what* means?"

Language can be a touchy subject in our relationship. He's a white, Southern-born linguist and "World Languages" teacher, and I'm an immigrant. He's theory; I'm praxis. I told him once, tipsy, "You learned languages because it was cool. I learned them to survive."

It is when I burn my wrist pulling a cookie sheet out of the oven that I actually hear myself. I hear another fugitive language, another part of this fugitive love: "Ukinana!" The saltiest of words because, for one, it is from my estranged, mentally ill, criminal biological mother's northern dialect. It is also a word with no smooth contours, sonically or aesthetically. Write it in cursive and what you get is spike after spike, even at the tips of its supposedly round penultimate and ultimate vowels. Quadrisyllabic: each quarter a jab, a slit in the air, the *phup!* at the end of a slash. I *am* the dirty mouth in our little family of three, but this getaway word gets even me. It's a modest shock, this word's effect, but big enough to jolt me when I'm fixing a batch of sweets.

Was I just cursing in my mother's tongue?

Mother, mother tongue, motherland. I'm nowhere near any of them now. I'm where I've landed. I'm in the Carolinas, a decade into, oddly because we are both polyglots, an English-speaking marriage with a Carolinian who has loved me more keenly and tenderly and honestly than anyone I've ever considered as, or was ever obligated to call, family. Despite our shared area of expertise, *language*, we have failed to live beyond the strait that divides, maybe bridges, his Americanness from mine. We agreed with the rules of our environment: English is the baseline.

It's been almost just as long that I've been in this motherhood that feels much like swimming to the end of an infinity pool, paddling toward a Filipino identity with a child on my back, only to be pulled by the rip and the tide of Southernness, whiteness, the America that wants me to forget who it is exactly that I am and where it is exactly that I am from. How it is exactly that I sound. I drown a little so she doesn't. This is what droves of immigrant parents before me have done: submerge the past. But maybe this is wrong.

I ask myself often, *Can I be a good person if I don't know myself?*

So many of us Filipinos are self-sacrificing. It's how we were raised: to be collectivist, of service to everyone but ourselves. At your service, ma'am, sir.

Back home—in the otherworld—people also like to say, "Ang 'di lumilingon sa pinanggalingan, 'di makakarating sa paroroonan." The person who doesn't look back to their origins will not arrive at their destination.

I tried to look back. I wrote a memoir: a childhood written in translation, mostly in English, for a "loosely" defined, which means narrowly selected or favored, American audience. The very act of writing memoir is its own translation work: from the experienced to the remembered and the accounted, from then to now, from life to art, from me to you. In the case of my debut book, it was also a practice in translation from one tongue to another, from there to here, from a *that* to a *this* that are inequivalent, much like how Lucy Sante describes her work and life in the essay "Lingua Franca":

> In order to write of my childhood, I have to translate. It is as if I were writing about someone else. As a boy, I lived in French; now, I live in English. The words don't fit, because languages are not equivalent to one another.

Although English is our trade and instruction language, as the Philippines was purchased by the United States from Spain (along with the Panama Canal and Puerto Rico), and we became twice-colonized, then anglicized, and in many aspects, made capitalist and America-obsessed, our English back home has always had its own inflections, intonations, prefixes, suffixes. We greet our teachers and elders with "Good morning, po." Perhaps our most spoken words are—because food is the center from which all Philippine life emanates—Sige, eat na. Dangling like an earring in the lobe of the listener's ear, or like the soft knob at the back of the speaker's throat, Tagalog is the inflection, the finish, our primal (though not first since there isn't a unifying, national "first") language that cups English where it spills, cinches, or tethers it where it is loose, or urges it out when it can't say what it means to say, as in "Basta, I don't know myself na." As a little girl obedient to and enamored by my nanny, who only spoke in Tagalog and Bisayâ to me, I spoke in more Tagalog than what my upper-classmates, or our classist society, preferred. Once, a girl taller and lighter-skinned than me bent down to my face and mocked me: "Can. You. Under. Stand. My. English. Or. Are. You. Dumb?"

That was the first time I felt ashamed of my mother tongue, of sharing something with my working-class and beloved nanny, whom my parents could no longer afford after their professional and political demise but who stayed as long as she could without pay to look after me. It was the first time I was bullied into forgetting my nature and my nurture, perhaps my first departure from self.

After the bullying, I removed Tagalog from my conversations, my lexicon. I was a budding writer, competing in middle school English-language essay contests and English-language spelling bees to secure my lot in an exclusive, all-girls, proudly Spanish-founded, American diplomat family-friendly (whew!) private school that my parents could not afford. Language had always been about survival. I represented the school in Scholastic teen writing competitions, the local newspaper's annual student issue, and intercollegiate social science and history debates. Poor and dark and short, in other words unwanted by my colonized social networks and "support" systems, all I had to offer was language, stories. English. Thought, spoken or written, was my adopted currency. To keep it—*me*—valuable or useful, like a foreigner having cash converted at an airport kiosk, I exchanged *pwede* for "can," *ikaw* for "you," *intindi* for "understand," *ako* for "me." *Can you understand me?*

And so it became always that: Was whatever I was writing or saying intelligible to whomever I was speaking to? Was it English enough? American enough? To make things worse, in early 2003, I was plucked from my adolescence in Metro Manila and pin-dropped by adoption to a rich family and an insular high school in Long Island, New York—what would be the genesis of a perennial exodus from my sampaguita-smelling, Pearl of the Orient home. A constant departure from my sampaguita-smelling, pearl-in-my-father's-palm self.

I've taken on a few evening writing courses so I can slowly dip back into the literary world, and a core lesson I teach in these workshops is on audience and awareness—that whomever you perceive yourself to be speaking to shapes what you notice, know, maybe even feel. They shape your art, which is to say, they shape you.

Part of this workshop exercise is to have students write down a list of six people who make up their audience. I give them five minutes to think on these select few, these message recipients, these people on the other end of the imaginary thread. I say, "If you appeal to everyone, you will matter to no one." I have them visualize, when the whisper or the scream or the stutter is sent, whose ear is poised to the hollow of the tin-can telephone. *Hello? Who's there?*

Individuals in these classes, no matter their writing level or publishing record, are always so moved by this part of the exercise. They begin their lists and hold back tears of joy, as if they've been waiting to not have to be all, for all. A decluttering of the psyche, a cleansing breath. A collective sigh. A break of sweat to cool down the body. They list their partners or spouses, their children or parents, the teacher who spurred them on, or the teacher who shut their aspirations down. The occasional neighbor, spiritual adviser, or hairstylist makes the cut.

But someone they fail to list, as I point out at the activity's surprise turn, is themselves.

I ask them, "Is your name on that list? Perhaps this is something to consider."

And soon after I ask this, I ask myself silently if I am being a hypocrite. I hope, however the writing looks or comes nowadays, I am writing to myself.

Dispatches from Recovery

2023

Today was a good day for a first visitor, for someone to bring me what I still know is my favorite Filipino dish: sinigang. She has brought me this and Filipino stories and Filipino humor, and her Filipino laugh that harmonizes with the sound of mine. Anya, neuroscientist and friend. Anya, fellow Filipina in coastal Carolina.

You wouldn't know we once shared a home, as in a city, as in a country . . . not right away. Where the Southern sweetens my talking, some Midwestern bumps up her words. You wouldn't know it right away even if you claimed you had a good eye for these things: the difference in our eyes, the shades of our skin, how my hair color is lighter. But when she starts reading a seemingly serious, unexpectedly naughty story, and I start gasping and laughing and I am all gums and teeth and she can't go on because her jaw has hit the floor, then you know. You know that some things can only be funny to us and those like us, as in like us who uprooted, like us who make a life here now, like us who've made careers and secured lots in our fields, even though often in those fields just being ourselves feels like a load of extra work.

I wonder if, in her field, she's looked at brains like mine, as in like hers, as in fluent in English and Tagalog and Immigrant. As in busy working mom. As in we tried. As in tired. You'd think she's come here to look at my scans or ask about diagnoses and prognoses, but no. She's come here to sit right under the clock, right where she blocks my view of it, and to speak in our shared tongue, expectant not only of my still having the ability to understand it but to speak it as well. I might be two seconds too late or two seconds too soon, but when she reads me a soft-pornographic short story that renders me speechless at the cleverly inserted kink, I feel like I feel when Stephen and I mirror each other's kindness or when Anouk says with no preface whatsoever "MA, LOOK!" *and wiggles right in front of my face the week's loose tooth. That is, I feel the two seconds part, one from another, giving me room to walk through to the now.*

4

The Net Effect

April 2021
My first travel-magazine writing assignment for ***Coastal Living***

In January 2021, it felt like it came out of nowhere: the invitation to write for a well-known travel magazine. But I know exactly where it came from. I'd started the new year by attending a yoga class at which we were told to set an intention: to find a word to commit to these next twelve months. Right there on my sweaty rubber mat, I chose a word I'd never liked but somehow always knew I needed. The word was *trust.* Having lived through a pandemic, I felt I had two options: waste more of my precious time toiling over what-ifs or adopt a way of life that invited and welcomed some kismet. *Trust,* as I breathed in. *Trust,* as I breathed out and transitioned to the next pose. One word was all it took to—like most of my friends who'd made major life changes the past couple of years—quit my toxic, twisted NGO job and allow myself to believe in the good that awaited me. I made a plan, a wish, really, on the mat: leave behind the office job and take on as many freelance writing, editing, and teaching gigs as I could and will my way to a forever and secret dream born at those early 2000s subway-station fixtures:

newsstands. As an undocumented teen in New York City, with the tips I got from my restaurant, nannying, and cleaning jobs, I bought travel magazines. I dreamt hard, because then it truly was just a dream. I didn't have the legal and financial means to travel. I had no passport, no state ID. And since there's no high like a savasana high, I finished the yoga class splayed on the mat while envisioning the crisp new passport I'd ask Stephen to help me apply for, and said to myself quietly, "I think I can, I think I can, I think I can. I can be the travel writer I've always wanted to be." Barely a month into what Anouk calls a lucky year ("Two twos!"), my trust bore fruit so sweet, it felt exactly like what sugar does to your brain: It changes mood, it alters behavior, it gives you something to be addicted to. An editor at *Coastal Living* magazine shot an email from her corner of the Universe to mine, asking me if I'd write a travel piece about living close to the water, and if that isn't providence writing its sweet name on my life, then I don't know what is.

From Coastal Living

We pull up to the dock early, as we both are wont to do in the unfamiliar. Sure, we both got "island time" in us: I'm from the Philippines, and Jason's from Tobago. But we also met through our better halves, both teachers who wrangle ten-year-olds all day and whose daily lives (sanity) rely on the structure of syllabi, the regularity of recess. We like them for this peculiarity: an inclination to keep time, track it. And today is not beyond marking milestones. It's our tenth fall as friends, our tenth year finding our place in this altogether familiar (for the tides, seafood, sherbet sunset) yet foreign (for the seersuckered luxe, mustard-based barbecue, unmistakable Charleston drawl) coastal town. Stephen and Sandy (Jason's longtime partner) work not far from here, where the peninsula's west side touches the eastern hem of the Ashley River and where we've all five pulled up in waterproof shoes and long sleeves today. We—Jason, Sandy, Stephen, now ten-year-old Anouk, and myself—came prepared, which is to say we came anxious. None of us have gone crabbing in these waters before.

Jason asks, "Ever go crabbing back home?"

I shake my head. "You?"

I hear the trepidation right away. "In Tobago, we catch crabs in mangroves under moonlight . . . with our hands." It's no wonder he's stuffed his trunk with a first aid kit and reflector vests. He says they're left over from his engineering job, but I think they're to buffer from the possibly friendship-ending activity I've signed us up for: Let's Go Crabbing, one of Airbnb's top four, best-rated experiences in the world. A decade has been plenty of time to not do as the locals do, and a receding pandemic means my days of cooping up in the confines of my home have whittled to somewhat of an end. With a world-renowned Gullah/Geechee crabbing coach right in our backyard (or should I say, backwaters?), there's really no excuse for us to dodge the sport any longer. To venture home, I first need to venture out.

Breaking up the morning's tension, Jason asks, "How do you cook crab in the Philippines?"

Ah, a welcome opportunity for me to unclench my toes and to divulge as I find most pleasurable. I list my sources of comfort: tamarind, cane vinegar, calamansi, coconut milk. Jason perks up upon hearing the last ingredient. Curry in coconut milk, he says, is the Tobagonian way of serving crab, a point of connection between us in a beach town where it's not always the easiest to put a finger on something that says home.

"If we catch some today, you're cookin'," I kid as one of our hosts approaches.

His name is Art Perry, and he says we're in for some rugged kind of fun. "No phones," he mutters as he takes my emotional-support device. I reach back for it. Snap, really. He clicks his tongue. "You're here to catch some crabs." Before I can protest further, he's already leading us down the pier, along which he's dropped nets—one of three ways we'll be catching South Carolina blue crab today. Three. I thought I signed up for *one* activity.

Art gives the protocol safety speech (speaking to all of us but staring at me) and checks for our fishing licenses (purchased through the Department of Natural Resources website earlier in the day, fees for which help fund maritime forest replenishment). He notes two legalities: captured egg-bearing females and all crabs measuring under five inches from spike to spike must be returned to the water. "The DNR," he says, "is always watching." He shares a couple of anecdotes about some delinquents and fines, emphasis on the former. I salute. We laugh. As he wraps up, Tia Clark eases in like a Carolina breeze, erasing all memory of my faux pas. Just having finished setting up lines and nets, she introduces herself, tells us the water's moving, temps are in the mid-sixties, and it's the best time to go crabbing. She asks, "So which one of you is the most scared today?"

I raise my hand, although I don't have to. Everyone already has their heads turned to me.

Tia says, "You're going first, then."

I watch her drape a cast net on her arm. She instructs I do the same just before I swing the contraption above the dock rails, away from the hardwood decking that could snag it, and onto the upstream from where the net will mushroom open, then billow to a close, hopefully catching hard-shell crabs full of sweet, brackish-water meat.

"I'm sorry?" I repeat a few times, first polite, then obliging, addled, unenthused. I consider my bad back (straightening it), bad wrist (giving it a flick), bad shoulder (giving it a rub). I remember that, while I planned this excursion, I remain a reluctant, decrepit traveler.

She cracks some jokes about five-year-olds who can do it, and I joke back. I do; I must. I've nothing but my humor left. With poise long gone, I take a rather audible breath. Art pulls his phone out to take a photo. The group gawks, cringes. Tia cheers me on. And I swing. I swing like my seafaring, island-dwelling ancestors are watching. The net pancakes into the air, lands on and breaks the water's surface, and swallows into itself whatever loiters beneath (shrimp, not crab, unfortunately). It was a near-perfect throw, or so I'm told.

"Did you see what you just did?" Tia yells, high-fiving me and beaming her wide smile.

"I . . . didn't. I closed my eyes."

She gulps air to stifle a laugh. "Doesn't matter," she says, flashing the shot Art snapped. "You did this."

And just like that, my confidence sparks out of her ability to make newbies feel like pros. I'm ready to try the cast net method again, or another.

Tia demonstrates how to use a drop net baited with chicken. She explains that the chicken neck, an unwanted part for human consumption, has been a bait of choice for the Gullah/Geechee, including her family, for hundreds of years. "Necks in the net; legs on the kitchen table," she says. "One's for feeding the crabs; the other, for feeding our families."

It's Jason's and Sandy's time to shine. With Sandy holding a pronged pole to keep the net's string away from the dock's jagged edge, Jason pulls up the net swiftly but gently so as not to alert the crabs of their capture. But there's no capture, not the first time. Tia assures us it's all right. The first pulls are mostly done to determine where the crabs are: closer to shore or deep and away. As Art moves the nets to shallower water, where it seems the crabs have gathered today, Tia calls us to regroup by the pier entrance. "Story time," she says.

As we walk, I decide that Tia is one of us. I sidle up to her to ask her a question I'd have no trouble asking myself, Anouk, or Stephen. "Tia! Tia, can I ask you something? What's the water telling you today?"

She grins, looks out. "That I needed to be here."

She doesn't speak again until we've all gathered, and what she shares next doesn't at all feel unrelated to the profundity she just so casually dropped on me. We learn about what brought her to the water in 2017: health problems, a reckoning with habits and vices, a nagging feeling that although she had spent her entire life in Charleston, a connection was missing. "I was losing it, and my cousin told me to get out on the water with him. I'd never gone crabbing before!"

I get a vision of me suffocating from work and pandemic homeschooling and general quarantine miasma, unspooling from years of cultural exile, also losing it and as well yearning to be in or by water.

Tia tells us that one crabbing experience led to another, and another. "I wanted to be next to the water every day. This water"—she points behind her—"breathed life back into me. How could I not take all my friends crabbing?"

She took coworkers, neighbors, and her wife, who didn't yet understand how Tia could stand in the heat, waiting, waiting, waiting for her line or net to catch dinner. "It was this new connection to water."

But was it new?

Growing up in downtown Charleston with Gullah/Geechee roots, it's an inequity that it took four decades for Tia to break the disconnect. Members of the Gullah/Geechee Nation have relied on subsistence fishing and crabbing for centuries, surviving their kidnapping from nations in West Africa and the prolonged and deliberate injustice ahead—clinging to each other and to an amalgam of languages, flavors, pieces of heritage, and home, including a long-standing dependence on fisheries and a deep respect for nature and the ocean. As their present tribal leader and nearby Beaufort resident, Queen Quet, is known to say in their creole tongue, "De wata bring we. De wata gwinne tek we bak." A reminder that people must live in harmony with the water.

Understanding that systems of government, law, economics, and logistics have all long deterred Black and other communities of color from water sports and sportfishing in the Lowcountry, I still want to hear why Tia believes it took her this long to discover the joy of crabbing. I ask and she volleys the question right back. "Well, why did it take *you* this long?"

I can make a joke or be forthright. Tia's gregarious but she's no-nonsense. "It's strange because I'm from an archipelago nation and this should totally be my thing but . . ."

Jason and Sandy pick up where I pause: Sportfishing is usually marketed to tourists, not locals. Water recreation is known as a luxury item for a sportsman of a certain kind, color. We're two immigrant-and-teacher pairings.

Boat landings and beaches here are, yes, progressively becoming more inviting, inclusive, but we have a ways to go. Tia nods and chimes in. "Airbnb flew me to their headquarters because they wanted me to teach other hosts how to get better reviews. I'm gay, Black, and over forty. This is not how life usually goes. And that's why I do it. I want people like me, like y'all, to know the joy of crabbing, that it can be this very everyday, casual thing."

I feel warm, and I'm not sure if it's because I've actually moved today, or because her joy, her honesty, her success (yes, that too!) make it evident that we've belonged for as long as the water has waited for us.

Art calls from down the dock. Anouk dashes to him, and they pull a drop net together, revealing a five-incher. She squeals, I squeal, a couple of boaters raise their thermoses to congratulate her. Tia teaches her how to press down on the shell and pin down the pincers, and she does it ever so confidently and proudly. The water is on our side, we know it. We scramble to drop nets near and far. Sandy and Jason get a catch, and another.

Riding this wave of excitement, Tia asks who's ready to try the hardest, perhaps least rewarding, of crabbing methods: handlining. Again, I raise my hand. Sandy does too, and we're on a joint mission. The first few tries garner nothing, but lo, the third time's the charm. She pulls, slowly, slowly, even slower, as Tia instructs, just above a whisper. And I pierce the water with my gaze, looking out for blue shells and claws. It's up to my poor vision and strong Filipino instincts now. I can't see very well but my gut says *Go!* I scoop down with a dip net, and there he is: measuring six inches across the back, meaty, feisty, the largest catch of the day. My catch. I yell, "Get that curry cookin', Jason!"

Later, it's a curried crab feast at Jason's house, at what he calls "Bago Shack." Tia will hand Anouk a metal cracker at a table covered in banana leaves and edible flowers to teach one last and essential lesson: how to crack and clean out a crab. Of course, in a matter of minutes, my daughter's fingers will turn yellow from Jason's homemade spice mix, and she will have already become less of an apprentice, more of a master. I'm proud. Of us. We're becoming native, to ourselves and to each other. To rest and recreation. I retrieve the mental picture I took at day's end on the dock. It's a tight shot of everyone sun-tired and grinning, a reflection of my own wide and toothy smile caught in a frame of Tia's sunglasses. It's an image I'll want to send to the leisure-averse and apprehensive woman I've been since moving to coastal Carolina, along with a message I've yearned to say to her these ten years: *Wish you were here.*

PART II

BAGGAGE

Charlotte Douglas International Airport,
Charlotte, North Carolina
Unceded Catawba, Cherokee, Coharie, and
Lumbee Land
Puerto Rico, la Isla del Encanto
Charleston, South Carolina
Unceded Edisto Natchez-Kusso Land

—*Late 2021–Mid 2022*

Dispatches from Recovery

2023

I'm not supposed to be here. I was just on assignment for a travel story for a dream magazine. I'm not supposed to be routinely getting blood drawn and routinely having my brain scanned and routinely having my urine measured against my liquid intake. I'm not supposed to be screaming for ice for my head and a heating pad for my back and MORE MEDS! I need them NOW, please! I was supposed to be writing the second half of the travel essay that's due to my editor next week. (Does anyone know where my laptop is? I didn't leave it at the café, did I?) Anouk should be getting ready for her twelfth birthday party at the skating rink, not running to the end of the hall where the nurses' station is, asking for more ice, a fresh heating pad, and the next round of pills for her mama. Stephen should be packing right now, last-minute packer that he is, getting set for our Thanksgiving trip to London and not talking to Anya on the other side of the door that's blocking her view of me writhing in pain. He tried to pull the door behind him, but it didn't close all the way. I can hear their concerns. Their love. He tells her that sometime in the middle of the night, I took a turn and woke up presenting signs of meningitis.

"MENINGITIS?!" I hear Anya yelp.

Stephen uses his low-and-slow way of talking to comfort her. (He is always comforting everyone here, even the nurses, even the doctors.) "Not meningitis but like it," he says.

It's the blood. The same blood that fed on the gray loops on the hind side of my skull. Same blood that turned something into nothing, the all of it to the none of it. Same blood that swirled in my head while I was trying to write a travel essay at a café, swirled so much it made my world spin. Now it's coming for my neck and my spine, and I feel what liquid does to the supposedly solid parts of me. Head strong. Strong back. Weight of the world on her shoulders. Heart like a truck. This is who people say I am in the cards they write and in the messages they send. Who I am. Or who she is, the person I may or may not be a placeholder for.

"Mama, I have it," Anouk says as she holds an ice pack to my forehead. And again with no preface whatsoever: "Remember the Philippines, Mama? Remember the starfish? Remember the pool in Puerto Rico? Remember? Mama? The jellyfish in Jamaica, Mama?"

Remember. Remember.

I do as she says, and I close my eyes. I close my eyes and go to these places. I go to these places, and I hear the waves. I hear the roosters. I go; I close my eyes and go. I watch where I step, make sure there aren't jellyfish in my way. I take off without so much as a "See you later" or goodbye.

5

Priority Boarding

I am here. They are there. Between us is a glass door, full-body thermal screener, digital scanner for boarding passes, and an airline agent who is staring me down. This gelled-up man pulls his mask down to his chin, as if doing so would help him see me better, understand what it is I think I'm trying to do. Twice, he snaps his fingers. "Ma'am. Ma'am! Here."

I don't move, don't speak. He calls again, and I give him the slightest of headshakes. I still don't move toward him. I can't. I am held in place by the five pieces of luggage with me. "Ma'am! I need to speak with you. Please!" the agent yells. Everyone who tries not to stare does stare. I look around, back at them who are concerned but trying not to be. I feel like a child again, my siblings who've also just been scolded now watching me endure.

"I'm . . ." is all that leaves my lips, the polymer of my KN95 mask.

The agent goes in and out of spite stories, heading his solo noise barrage from behind the help desk, his frustration with my lack of cooperation now diffused to a general chagrin at an airportful's failure to comply. He types fast, every clack giving sound to the gall that's balled up in him for the past, oh, I don't know, hour and a half that the airport has been in service this morning. In his eyes, humanity is a failure, and at its lowest level is me, a woman with too many bags. One more hard, emphatic click on the keyboard, and he slaps boarding passes at the desk, because that's it, that's all the time he'll give me to walk over. When he leaves his station, eyes follow him until something else draws their attention. They look the other way, far behind me, where, from what I can hear, is someone official with a two-way radio.

I talk low, try to send a message underground. "Stephen, look at me. Look this way."

The glass door continues to separate us. He's not hearing me. He's also looking down to where his foot is meddling with the wheelchair pedal he hasn't quite figured out. The wheelchair attendant provided by the airport is head down at the top of the ramp with a clipboard, checking this, checking that. He's left the wheelchair and the grown and grumbling man in it in the middle of the ramp, making my father-in-law a two-hundred-plus-pound obstruction to first-class passengers now allowed to board. Just minutes ago, we—me, Anouk, Stephen, and his parents—were a convoy rolling and roiling through Charlotte Douglas, kicking up a dust storm and infecting other passengers with our collective agita. So much huffin' and puffin', so much anxious hummin' to the tune of a car dealership campaign jingle.

It's Anouk's first time outside the fifty states, Stephen's and my first time traveling with his parents since a blowout six years ago, and his parents' first grand and needy opportunity to display to us a new side of their low-frequency but high-intensity good ole American fear. To make travel anxiety more baneful, his dad twisted an ankle a week ago and is only mobile by way of snarking at whoever is closest to him or the wheelchair. Today that ever-so-lucky person is Stephen. I'm watching him unsuccessfully unlock the pedal, the feeling of having disappointed his father made plain by his pigeon-toed stance. His mom is patting the air with one hand, calming down her husband, who is miffed and has got his signature scowl to prove it. They're all four stuck on the midway to our plane, and Anouk is, or at least her arm is, stuck to her grandmother because, Mimi believes, children get stolen at these peopled places all the time. I want to rescue her from my mother-in-law's grip, but I am stuck here, and with me are three too many things that are not registered in my name.

"Ma'am, do all these suitcases belong to you?" the agent asks.

The officer mumbling to a radio circles me like a hawk. Of the four suitcases in my grip and the weekender at my elbow, only two belong to me.

I know from previous times I've been stopped, approached, questioned, or apprehended that I should always tell just enough of the truth. "No, sir, they're not." Before COVID and after marriage, I was always stopped at airports, no matter where I was going, what I was wearing, what was on me, or whom I was with. I was, ten times out of ten, patted down. Every flight to and fro became practice. Eventually, I learned to conjure détente. I acquired a language of studied compliance, facial expressions, mannerisms. The less I yawned or sighed, the less likely I was to cast a spotlight on myself. I kept my eyes looking exploratory, like a tourist's, but never alert, like a child who's just crayoned the wall. I played peekaboo with strangers' babies but never hid my face with a hat. When traveling with Stephen, I always asked for a kiss just before we were called, *Next.* Calibrations like these lowered the frequency of pat-downs, from a ten to a seven, and while they didn't eliminate the need for me to always, *always*, check in and print boarding passes in person and with a person, they shortened the very forced "congenial" conversations with agents and officers who were only chatting me up so they could buy time to look me up.

Stephen learned the ways too. He revved up the politesse, gave away compliments not so much like candy but like an it's-on-me scoop of Chipotle guacamole. He read name tags and ended his sentences with agents' and officers' names. We're practiced, or we were. I'm learning at this moment that the pandemic has made us rusty: at hellos, at goodbyes, at surviving the time and space between.

The agent and officer exchange looks, speaking the language of glances. The agent flips over and reads the ticket on one of the suitcases. "I'm gonna need your boarding pass and ID."

Before marriage and mastering airport protocols together, it was four years of dating and dodging checkpoints. No flying for me, no dancing at ID-only clubs, no getting off the subway if cops were set up with fold-away tables on the station platform. Other couples we knew earned the intimacy of routine by navigating their way through decisions on which takeout place or weeknight movie. But for me and Stephen, the choices were, because we mostly dated long-distance: me on an overnight Amtrak or Greyhound or him on a flight we afforded by skipping meals. When we applied for a marriage license at New York City Hall in my seventh year as an undocumented person, I was called to and sequestered in a back room and questioned about my failed naturalization through transnational adoption, my lack of a Social Security number, and my only ID being an expired Philippine passport. For over an hour in that clammy room I thought it was the last I would see of Stephen, that I would get deported. I was okay with saying goodbye to America but not to him. Separated by a door, my and Stephen's answers matched. Our love proved to be telepathic. They let me go after some time and released us a cellophane-thin license to wed.

Sharing a weak iced coffee on a park bench and not speaking about what we had just gone through, we had an understanding that afternoon that, despite my being independent and determined and clever and my experience working for an immigration lawyer, it wouldn't be the last time I would need him to speak on my behalf or vouch for my identity. Marriage, or more accurately taxes filed jointly after marriage, bore me permanent resident immigration status, then American citizenship, but it did not ensure smooth departures or swift procedures. I've had a hunch that my civil violation of having been undocumented means my name is flagged in some system, and a way to correct it is to acquire a redress number from Homeland Security, but who has got the time?

"I have my ID but not my boarding pass."

"Are you boarding this plane?"

"Yes."

"Then you need to have a boarding pass."

"I have one, but he has it." I point to Stephen, who has, thanks to his patient finagling, unlocked the mystery of the wheelchair pedal. Now, if only he'd turn this way and help me solve the mystery of the five articles of luggage. No longer stranded on the purgatory of a ramp, he picks up his bag from the floor and begins to wheel his father forward when Anouk pulls at the hem of his shirt. *Mom,* I see her mouth move. *Of course, duh,* his body says as he shakes himself out of the paralysis of his father's sustained, spellbinding anger. When he turns to see if I'm at the top of the ramp, I'm not there at all. I'm here, on the other side of the glass, a Ping-Pong ball between an airline agent who wants me and my two, and only two, things on the plane and a TSA cop who wants to know why two, and only two, of these effects are tagged to correspond to a barcode on a boarding pass that is not, "So sorry, Officer, I can explain," in my possession.

"My husband is coming with my pass."

~

Four Christmases ago, I was shopping at our neighborhood Harris Teeter for tea, bread, and gift-wrapping tape when a cashier, white and in late middle age, threatened to confiscate my credit card and called security on me. In line after two white women with cartfuls of groceries and kitchen appliances, I was paying with a credit card like they had just nonchalantly, easily paid for their bags and bags of goods with their credit cards. I came to the store at the end of a walk-run, still sweaty in my pocketless spandex, and had only stuffed into my sports bra a credit card and my phone.

"I'm gonna need your ID," the cashier said before tallying up my items.

"Oh, I just went for a jog, gosh. I don't have my purse on me." I was still smiling, yet to realize what was going on. "Is that okay?"

"No ID, no groceries." She looked behind her to another cashier who looked just like her, teased bangs and all. They gave each other a look of agreement, then excitement. I was, to them, their catch.

"It's tea and bread. And tape. Are you serious?"

"I can't be certain this card is yours, ma'am." She turned around again to her colleague, her accomplice.

I understood. I said again, slowly, emphatically, "It's tea. And bread. And tape. I am paying with *my* card."

"Ma'am, we get a lotta theft this time of year." She said it so loudly, everyone in line behind me and at nearby registers looked our way. "You don't look like a Barnes."

"What do I look like, then? What do those women look like, the ones who were just here paying for an Instant Pot with a credit card? You didn't check their IDs."

My credit card still in her grip, she pursed her lips and shook her head. "You leave me no choice, ma'am. I'll have to keep this until you can prove it is yours."

"Might hafta call security," her sidekick said.

I kept swallowing air and my spit to keep myself from bursting into tears. Everyone was looking at me as Christmas music and holiday deal announcements blared from the speakers. I could hear people behind me sigh in exasperation, my little nonissue stalling their holiday shopping. As I texted Stephen in all-caps and misspellings—SOS PLS COME HARRIS TEETHER QUICK CASHIER LINE 6 BRING MY ID IN BLACK MADE WELL PURSE ASAP—shoppers rolled away from lane 6 to another open register. A manager and a security guard arrived from opposite ends of the store, and they let the honcho and her aide explain my being a tea and bread and gift-wrapping tape thief.

Their accusations swirled up to the fluorescent-lit ceiling, mingling with songs about Christ's birth and daily deals on honey-baked ham. It was just another all-American Christmas. It didn't matter that we were a blue Dem dot in a red GOP state. I was, yet again, in the eye of a twister, and to stay alive all I had to do was stay incredibly still. I had two choices in that moment: explode already or add this fuse to the growing, ticking time bomb in me. I could hear my heartbeat in my ear and feel heat rise from my core to my neck. The manager was asking me questions, but I continued to ignore him and stare at the tea and the bread and the tape on the conveyor belt. I imagined myself sipping milky tea and dipping my bread in it, the way we sometimes do back home. I could have asked him if it was even legal to confiscate my credit card, but I didn't. I was the tea bag steeping in hot water; the longer the steep, the stronger the brew.

Within minutes, Stephen arrived with first-grader Anouk but without my ID or my black Madewell purse. He was still in the school carpool line when I texted, and he decided that coming sooner was more helpful than driving five minutes home for my bag and another five minutes to the store. He knew the awful truth: His face was enough of an ID. Upon his arrival, neither of us can remember the exact mechanics of how my credit card was released, my items rung and summed and bagged up, and my alleged theft dropped. I had a few more errands to run and small gifts to buy from other stores at the same strip mall. For every one, I made him queue up and pay while I waited outside with Anouk, faking a smile and holding back tears while I asked her about recess, lunch, and her favorite part of the day.

~

We're well on our way down the ramp and into the plane, just like we were well on our way out of Harris Teeter and to the other stores. We're failing at pretending that nothing just happened. I'm snapping at Stephen, just under my breath, about walking ahead so fast without me and the suitcases. He's mumbling back in an even lower volume and tone, apologizing for not just the luggage situation and the boarding pass situation but the baggage of this particular trip. Family vacations are not just journeys to other places but time warps to a chapter of life when you might have been without power, without the right words, without the knowledge or understanding or acceptance of self that you worked so hard to have but can suddenly lose today and therefore be outside your adult self and back inside the delirium of a parent's displeasure. You are so caught up in the dismal air that you grew up breathing that you are not breathing at all. Instead, you are so choking on words like *Yessir* and *Be right there* that you leave behind your life partner—the one you saw on a rooftop somewhere and with whom you wanted to spend your life, catching tadpoles, and who packs you burn cream because your white skin can't handle the sun—and let her attract every chance of being stopped, questioned, with demands for proof of identity. Of her existence.

Farther down the ramp, Anouk pulls her purple suitcase behind her. She's already forgotten, I think, about what she just watched through the glass: me, encircled by two men with different powers in equally blue uniforms. Excited for the water park and *three* resort pools, she's got a little skip to balance out her little limp. She turns around, all smiles. It's her first big trip. So we smile back, maybe even fake a handhold. We're on this trip to test the waters of travel so that I can coax my way home. It's not a good start, but I hold on to the feeling of possibility I found while crabbing. *Wish you were here.* I slide into my plane seat and immediately plug in my headphones. I select the tab for my favorite category of in-flight movies: horror. My headphones are noise-canceling. I am in another scary but preferred world now, away from the nearby familial terror. Stephen, in the aisle seat, reaches across to hand his parents extra masks I've packed in his carry-on. It looks like the flight attendant has minded their exposed faces. I choose not to join in on the fuss. I will protect my and Anouk's time. I press Play. We take off. I enjoy the show.

DISPATCHES FROM RECOVERY

2023

There are two things you don't want when you're staying at a hospital: a power outage and a fire. But of course, adding specific insult to actual injury, a hospital generator has burst into flames. The alarm system is blaring and purple and red lights are flashing, and to protect me—my hearing, my seeing, my brain—the white woman I call my mother-in-law has her hands cupped over my ears and her torso leaning forward forty-five degrees to me like a shield. She sings, "I've got peace like a river, I've got peace like a river, I've got peace like a river in my soul." My favorite line from the only hymn I still sing. It's a song she knows, and the fact that I still know it too (and had requested her to sing it to help calm me down) is the middle ground between her rural Carolinian conservatism and my progressive, agnostic, humanist views, whatever all of that means.

The neuro unit is on lockdown, meaning even if we tried to run, if I could run, we'd just circle right back to my beige-and-white room. But I'm a planner, is what I remember, so gesture at the linens cart I do. "That," I say to my mother-in-law, "is how you'll roll me out of here should you need to." She looks at the pile of hospital laundry, then back at me, and continues her singing.

She's grounding both of us now, I see. I can feel her breath on my face, can smell the Dove products she uses, and I hear the inhales from when she pauses between "river" and "I've got peace." It's coming to me now that this is the closest we've been ideologically since the pandemic exposed and heightened our differences and the closest we've been physically since our holiday in Puerto Rico. In my time of need, and Stephen's and Anouk's, despite my inability to remember who I am truly and fully and to know where I am in time and space exactly, there was comfort found in her offer to hold tonight's vigil and give my two their well-deserved and much-needed break.

6

La Isla del Encanto

December 19, 2021

It hits me right away. The heat embraces me and being here just feels so right.

Puerto Rico and the Philippines are sisters from the same colonizing patriarchies. Spain first, the United States after. *The Catholics handed us over to the Protestants for a measly $20 million in 1898,* is how I've taught the two countries' twin fates to Anouk. Some houses in California cost more than that, I explain to her. "So, you'd think with that kinda bargain, they'd have relief funds ready for us after natural disasters." She's got a curious gait, a right side in need of strengthening, and reading comprehension needs, but you can't fool her with a mass-produced textbook. Some parents prepare their children for travel by downloading a new iPad movie. I gird mine with history.

"They look alike, Bitty," I say, pointing out the shuttle window. The forest, el bosque, holds a biodiverse mystery on one side of the road.

It's code: The two countries suffer alike, thrive alike. Not always, but many times they do and in many similar ways. As much as I'm readying myself for a long-awaited homecoming, I'm readying her too. Beauty and truth, they go together like her two neurodivergent parents, like Harpoon the bunny and Beeks the house cat. Meaning, it's easier to comprehend one without the other, but it's their pairing that turns them into story. I'm thinking now of our wedding ceremony. We fused Filipino customs of coin exchanging, lighting candles, binding by a cord, and a shared marital veil with Presbyterian hymns and blessings. They were customs I had grown up with and rituals Stephen was raised on, but together we gave new meaning to them. In the aughts, we didn't yet have words like *deconstruction* and *reconstruction*, but we got the gist.

We arrive at El Conquistador Resort, and nervous laughter escapes through my clenched teeth by way of a single, strangulated wheeze.

"Cringe," Anouk says in her new tween parlance, and I think, *Exactly.*

"It's too good. What a wild sense of humor God has," Stephen says under his breath after some small talk with and tipping the driver. His parents leave us with the bags—off they go to the lobby. They couldn't have paid for a more ironic vacation. Gearing up for come what may, Stephen mumbles, "Here we go."

I give him my assurance: an air kiss and "See you at the pool bar."

Like on the plane, I don't want to join in on the fuss of checking in. I let Stephen help his parents, who insist he be by their side at all times because "We don't speak Spanish" and to whom he explains that almost everyone here, especially at the resort, speaks English. Instead of following them as they make toward the lobby, I pull Anouk to the courtyard just ahead of the valet. I'm already having second thoughts about this trip, but she runs ahead of me, following the movement of the sun. Her excitement resets me.

"MAMA!" Even with her mask still on, I can tell she's smiling.

I tell her it's okay to take off her mask because we're outside, so she pulls hers down to her chin. When I make it to the banister she's folded her body over, I pull her back by her shirt. "Okay, careful, careful."

She steadies, places both feet back on the ground.

"Pretty, right?"

"MOM!" It's all making sense to her, all the times I've said that despite how lucky and privileged we are to live close to a beach, there's still a kind of blue she has yet to see. "MA!" She goes on like this, monosyllabic and breathless, until afternoon becomes evening.

After getting our temperatures taken at the front desk, we roll our suitcases to our room and unzip them. She changes into her rashguard so fast, I have to keep up and finish tying the sash on my swim skirt in the elevator. Meanwhile, Stephen continues to lag in the past. He takes a quick nap. He'll keep napping throughout our vacation but never be rested. These become the two speeds of our holiday, the two storylines I toggle: a ten-year-old not quite running but speed walking *(Safety first, Mom!)* from pool to pool, and a thirty-five-year-old decelerating, U-turning, and parking himself back where the need for getting lost in his mind was born.

La Isla del Encanto has made her look outward, and she's constantly pointing and yelling, "MOM! MA!" Like I hoped travel would do, it is growing her insight, her love. It is giving back to her kinesthesia and synesthesia she's been robbed of for a period that's now been nearly a quarter of her life. Meanwhile, travel, or traveling under different circumstances, has cast a different spell on Stephen. For a time in college, he stayed a semester in PR to practice the language and, I think, bound even farther away from home. He was looking forward to returning to the magic, or at least the hiding place it became. Maybe he hoped that after all these years, he could say, "Look, here's a side of me that I hope won't invite your ire, Dad, and won't stoke your fears, Mom." But no, being here proves to be his least favorite kind of anathema. People do get too set in their ways, and even travel can't change them.

The elevator dings, and its doors open to wet air. Like my love for a dear someone whom I know isn't at their best, this air is everywhere and heavy.

"Ma! Summer in December!"

I nod, even though it feels more like late spring. I'm happy for her, but sad for him. Two things can be true at once, like this island's beauty and the many literal and figurative hurricanes it's still recovering from. Anouk and I step out of the elevator and head to the largest of the pools, and on this short, slowed walk, I recall what a friend's immigrant mom had said about traveling, immigrating, and moving, and I'm negotiating in my mind about how true or untrue it is, or both: *Wherever you go, and there you are.*

Dispatches from Recovery

2023

The thing about the woman who is my mother-in-law is that when distanced from what I recall was her Protestant shame and American fear, even if that means being trapped on an intensive-care floor just eight stories above a hospital cafeteria fire, she quickly becomes the most delightful company. For one, the woman can cook. Her casseroles are a nice break from sweaty hospital meat. For another, she has the gentlest disposition and most soothing voice (thanks to the hymnals she's practiced from for nearly seventy years). Apart from her husband, her worries fade, perhaps not away but from front and center, and her only care and the precious subject of her attention becomes y-o-u. That if told to evacuate the building, she will, with her rheumatic knuckles and her dimming peripheral vision, boost me onto a heap of hospital linens and convey me through the hospital's guts and out its mouth and onto a Charleston cobblestone street. I tell her, little shaky voice that I have, that this is the plan, and we are silent for a moment before pure hysterics take over. And we laugh like this, as though I weren't hooked up to prompters and lifesaving, pain-killing fluids and as though her quadrennial voting habits didn't make life harsher and saltier and more perilous for a Brown woman like me.

At the moment, yes, we are confronted by an emergency and could be consumed by fire. But at the moment, too, although I remember that we are often confronted by our differences, we also can very well be consumed by each other's love. My wish is that along with recovering my health and my place in this life, soured relationships will also sweeten with time, that my hope will be restored not just for and in myself but for and in others too. And in the process, I hope she'll feel the privilege of caring for me. Because rebuilding me and my world—and we'll need much help from left and right and center—means growing and strengthening my capacity to stand for what is good and just. Suspended in this in-between recovery state with me, little does my mother-in-law know that she is a means to my healthier end, which is a means to a liberatory future for me, for my girl, and even for her, a woman I hope to move out from under the tyranny of a Southern husband and Southern heritage both stuck in regrets, resentments, and an unresolvable past and both benefiting egoistically and politically every time she allows her fears to narrow her mind and neither a part of the peace she calls out to when she sings.

7

Lazy River

Anouk and I are the first to board the first ferry for the day. Who knows where Stephen is? Seabirds swoop down to catch breakfast, a mast of nautical flags postures to catch the most wind. And this wind, it's gotten stronger since we boarded. My collar slaps at my neck; my hair swirls and whips. I pull my hair back into a bun. Anouk squints to protect her peepers. The waves, they're breaking fiercer. I get goose bumps. A little churn in my stomach signals I should look away, and I do. I turn the other way toward stillness, to the verdant slope where the casitas and four stories of the resort are lodged—and I consider the etymology of the word *lodging*, which originally meant "to have been placed." This is where I'm currently placed: a four-star seaside resort paid for by my in-laws, with whom I rarely agree and to whom I rarely defer unless it means taking advantage of such classy amenities. Sometimes, I'll take what my proximity to their privilege affords me. I'm Filipino, which means I know how to bargain. I am kind and cunning. I'm a shrewd human who'll use others' resources to power the movements I'm a part of.

Speaking of, I see a trio ambling downslope. While they are still so far away and to my vision remain in miniature, three dots worming down a path to a newly restored, post–Hurricane Maria dock, I know immediately who it is and what is slowing them down besides the twisted ankle and the steepness of the slope. I can feel Stephen's anguish from here. I avert my eyes and set them farther up the rambling coastline, trace it so far along I might just get a peek of El Yunque. I'll keep doing this to steady myself and settle my stomach, looking out to the distance and grandeur and then imagine what could be beyond or beneath, because for most of the trip, what will accompany Anouk, Stephen, and me, our very good team, will be no trifling concern over my in-law's paltry moods and never-ending gripes.

Among other things, Grandfather Grumpy will scoff at the cable-car attendant about mask wearing; the Dowager Downer will pitch to the Caribbean breeze doldrums about missing the cold and a chance at a white Christmas. The malaise will be persistent, but I will try my best to tiptoe around its prevalence. I will make the definitive choice to consider it less ubiquitous and more concentrated, which means I can keep it compact: something I can set aside. I will do just as my therapist has taught me to do when in uncomfortable family gatherings: disengage from the trigger and ground myself in a peaceful place, imagined or otherwise. I am not always quick to do what's right, but I am agile, nimble, teachable. Thank heavens my soulmates are too. Together, we are looking for better ways for anything and everything.

For the rest of our time on Palomino Island and in El Conquistador, I'll have equal parts mercy and intolerance for Stephen, and, like a sitcom mom to a sitcom dad portraying a modern American family, I'll let him know this in quick handoffs of piña coladas or bottles of sunscreen. He'll say something about how he detested vacations while growing up, that this was a mistake, and I'll respond, rearming him with memories of our long-distance dating days, of how they opened up chances to redeem the glory of road trips, of crossing boundaries. How our very good team can do very hard things, then recalibrate, optimize. If we can protect our house from pests and sewage flooding, we can swat at threats to our family's happy memory making and my rightful immigrant rest, no matter who paid for it or claims to have done so. *You should be thankful,* they might say, and we'll hurl it right back: You *should be thankful.* Stephen and I have spent our fifteen years together recovering from childhood and adolescent anxieties of many kinds, many of them related to forms of and questions on travel or mobility or identity.

I tell him, between sips of my mojito, that his parents' usual array of caustic verbal and body language, now overheard from a few palapas away, is no longer his life but just an occasional feature of it. And as the old adage goes, the present is a gift. We must accept it and inhabit it as fully as we can. At my most merciful, or perhaps tipsiest, I will reach from my side of the palapa to his, find his hand with my hand, and tell him without words but just with our quiet language that I need him to snap out of it, to redeem this vacation too, because it's not only a stop but a stepping stone to a much longer, weightier, infinitely more ambitious and cosmic journey.

~

This is what the resort water-park's lazy river teaches us: Just as there are ways through concrete for water to pass, there are ways around being too physically close to people who are making your holiday feel like a Monday in February. We makeshift a smaller vacation within the larger one, swirling off in our swimsuits and SPF to nether parts of the park. We go up forty-eight steps, by Anouk's count, to the top of the tallest speed slide. We go down: down the slide's massive vertical drop and into a pool that feeds water into other pools. We go even lower, deeper: an infinity pool eight feet deep but no impossible feat for my not-so-little swimmer. She and I choreograph a synchronized swim routine to a Dua Lipa song playing on endless repeat on resort speakers. When she and Stephen do "jumping challenges," the water displaces to a stream trickling around hammocks that I occasionally nap in. I watch them do every swan dive and scissor leap and helicopter over and over and over again, as secret childhood pool codes demand, and I resist the lulling swing of my hammock. My in-laws and their fetor are repelled by anything too fast, too cold, or too hot. "You sure you don't wanna come?" I say, even though I already know the answer. The super slides, the big pools in the shade, and the hot tubs overlooking the sea become sanctuaries.

We get our Stephen back. He and I break out of the brittle shells of his dejection and my disappointment. As a triune, we return to having a dimension that's anything but imperceptible. Our magic activated, we become the people that other guests watch for inspiration . . . because it's true: Nobody really knows how to "vacation." When we let want be our compass, we overdo it. When we let fear do the driving, it all becomes waste. In Puerto Rico, away from the very few people who truly are like North Stars to us—my best friends, my old editor, my longtime literary agent, Stephen's closest college friend—the three of us look to each other as coordinates on a map, fixing our gaze there and only there. We trust that to be in each other's orbit is to know our way around the sun.

Now we can have fun.

When I ask for a colada sans the piña and swirl in the mint leaf and melted ice leftover from my mojito, I set the new mode for poolside drinks: just sweet enough, fresh, and almost buttery, it's a mint chip ice-cream slushie for grown-ups that the other grown-ups copy.

When Anouk discovers that the warmest part of the largest pool is right between two wading platforms, she camps out there in some songful reverie, as other children watch and learn and slide in. Her glee is gravitational. I'm as enamored as her new playmates.

Stephen scouts the old Ping-Pong tables on the far end of the resort, the end still visibly untouched by contractors and post-hurricane investment money. We start our own mini tournament that attracts spectators who ask, in both English and Spanish, if they can join. Of course they can. It's rally after rally. Smiles upon smiles. Paddles get passed around. The group of table tennis enthusiasts grows, just nearing the limits of my pandemic times comfort. With a nudge of the elbow, my two understand. We've done our part. It's time to slink away to something else.

We keep slinking away to little discoveries throughout: a life-size chess game, two talking parrots. "Hola!" one says in a way that makes us think of our pets at home, how they might be at the door, waiting to greet us. We momentarily feel guilty for leaving them. When the cable car deposits us at the water-park entrance, lo and behold, a cat meets us at the gate. It loops around my leg and sits at my feet. I take it as a message my cat has sent me: He's all right, the bunny's all right, and I should go on having fun. It's up the forty-eight steps again, thundering down the super slide one, two, ten more times. This and the lulling of the seaside hammock create the contrasting textures of the final two of our four vacation days. We've released a smaller, truer holiday out of the stone of the larger one, evading my in-laws at the most advantageous times. This week, at this not-white Christmas, my immigrant innovation peaks.

But dinner's a different story.

Unlike breakfast, which we can rush through, or lunch, which has been poolside chicken fingers or pizza, or tostones on the go, dinner is sit-down, sit-together.

The marina at El Conquistador boasts what the website calls an open-air "seafood heaven," which means more chicken fingers for Stephen. He hasn't eaten fish since his first and last muddy Carolina fish fry as a child, so when I say our love is calamitous, I also mean we cross a culinary border. I was pescatarian when we met, but I proved to be weak against South Carolina mustard-based barbecue. Just as he was weak against, and eventually addicted to, the spice level I unabashedly declare at every Thai or Indian or Korean food order. I don't hold any kind of embargo on him for not having the palate or stomach for seafood, and he doesn't push dairy on me, knowing that it's sure to send me back to bed or many times to what the British more cutely call "the loo."

His folks are hungrier than us. They traded lunch for a nap. They've spent more time in their hotel room than anywhere else, and this very dinner is their vacation. We order appetizers and mains at once. The staff shortage is evident, though, especially at the resort's restaurants. I pick up on it. We're just dodging the Omicron wave in the States, and I don't doubt that there's a count for it here too. To be preemptive, I levee what I know will be quite a wait.

Bread, bread. I pass the bread basket around. I'm pushing carbs like it's life-changing, like it's the new Peloton. Everyone must try it. *Mmm, good bread. More bread?*

Everyone concedes. The basket is emptied and refilled. The little dish for butter is warm from passing hands. The little brown rolls spike up our sugar levels, and we're content, maybe even inclined to call this time "happy." Stephen's father is peppy; he waves our server over. Our server is a Puerto Rican man who used to live in Ohio, and he tells us what a beautiful family we are. He's mostly talking to my father-in-law. It's small talk about Cleveland and Cincinnati and some other airport they both hate flying out of. It's cool, congenial. There are even pats on the back. Our server asks if the three drinking adults—me, Stephen, and his dad—need more wine. "Por favor," Stephen and I say in sync.

"What would you be drinking if you were sitting in my seat?" my father-in-law asks.

Stephen and I exchange worried looks. It feels like a trick question. It tears a blip in the air; we hear the coqui just a little louder. I think of cutting in by switching my order from white wine to a negroni, but our server, he's stellar.

"Sir, you seem like you would enjoy the Lamborghini of margaritas."

"Tell me about this 'Lamborghini of margaritas,'" my father-in-law says in a way that makes us all hear the air quotes around the words. He's got his fingers threaded at his chest, like he's pleased to be thought of as this type of man.

The server describes it: top-shelf liquor after top-shelf liquor, the fishbowl it would come in, the bouquet of herbs and skewer of fruit to garnish it. He's clearly dealt with this kind of diner or drinker before, the kind who demands being impressed and needs the entire restaurant to turn around and hear it.

Stephen and I clock it, the irony of this drink. It's the drink of nondrinkers. We let it go.

The food still hasn't arrived when the luxury car of cocktails does. It's a bar in a bowl.

"Oo-hee!" my father-in-law blurts after his first sip. It's definitely strong, and I'm hoping it knocks him right out.

My mother-in-law's nap seems to have done her some good; she's not complaining about the not-white Christmas anymore. She loves the bread rolls. She tears them, takes every bite with her painted lips, rouge stamping the roll before it's inhaled. Her iced tea, an aperitivo to this ecumenical, seaside communion with a newfound relaxed self. I see her again in good light and feed her and the revelation. "More bread?"

Anouk's no longer at the age when she needs busying with crayons and tic-tac-toe on the place mat. She's just looking around, minding the starlight. Stephen's seated at the head of the table, opposite me, and he's got glassy eyes from his drink and a day in the sun. I slouch back, the deep V of my eyelet dress already revealing too much. No matter. It might turn out to be a good meal. I shall savor.

Twenty minutes in, there's no damage done to the Lamborghini. There's no feast before us either. Our server returns to apologize once again, and Stephen assures him in Spanish that we understand about the staff shortage. I say the same. As a thank-you, he squeezes my shoulder.

"Filipina?" he asks. In some places, I'm mistaken for Puerto Rican. In Puerto Rico, they peg me right. It's a compliment both ways, I think. He tells me about a Filipino friend from his old job in Ohio; I tell him about a proudly Boricua writer-friend. We go back and forth like this, acknowledging our connections. When I note how our people cook pork the same way, our *lechon* to their *lechón*, he squeezes my shoulder again. Somehow he knows I'd be okay with it, this kind of contact with a new acquaintance. But he's got more tables to attend to, and I've already stolen much of his time. I know he's one of only two servers on shift.

Pivoting, he says, "Volveré, esta vez con comida."

"Ey, ey, take our picture," my father-in-law interrupts. He unlocks his Samsung.

Our server obliges and reaches for the phone, gingerly.

"I can set a timer," I say.

"No, no, he'll take it. He's got nothing else to do. There's no food to serve. I mean, look around."

The comment steals Anouk's attention away from the starlight. Without turning her head, she peeks at our server through the corners of her eyes. I know what she's thinking. I place a hand on her lap.

I clear my throat. "I can—"

My father-in-law gets a word in before I'm able to finish. "Do. You. Know. How. To. Use. This. Phone?"

Stephen, Anouk, and I sit mortified. Our brains download the information: *This is rude and unacceptable.* The synapsing produces a backlog. Stephen is a teen again, hearing insults about his basketball performance at dinner. Anouk's eyes gloss over, and she's in some neutral space where bunnies sleep and cats purr. *No. Don't leave me. No, no,* I think.

I think.

I try to think.

"Argh, my contact!" I drop to the floor and pat it for a contact lens that is still, I hope nobody can tell, wrapped around the curve of my eyeball.

"Oh dear," my mother-in-law sighs.

"Eh? What happened?" her husband asks.

"She's lost her contact, honey."

"Heh?"

"Her con-tact. She's lost her con-tact. I never could use them, these contacts."

"Me neither, could never."

They go on, distracted. It buys the server a moment to escape.

My white dress flounced around me, I am an upside-down lily in the murky pond of this tired family dynamic. I'm head down in the water, fishing for an antidote. As I pretend to search for a thumbnail of silicone hydrogel, what I'm really looking for is a way out for our very good team, a way out of this place and time. "Help, guys! Careful where you step!" I shriek, knowing they'll respond. Their paralysis ends. They return to the here and now, to me. Stephen and Anouk drop to the floor and follow me under the white table linen. I swish at the air to halt their floor patting. I sign with my hands, *I'm okay*. I point to my eye, then mouth the words: *It's right here.*

Stephen grins. He's always loved that I'm quick and clever. He mouths, *I'm sorry.*

I shrug. He stays on the ground and goes on pretending to be in search of something other than the sense of dignity he loses every time he's around his father. The white linen becomes a kind of force field that shields him from come what may. Without words and just with my elbow, I tell him, *Come up for air only when you're ready.* I pull myself and Anouk out from under, dust off my dress, and excuse us. I tell the table that I'm lucky to have packed extra lenses in my carry-on. She and I circle around the marina to the host desk, where I find our server rightfully sharing details of the encounter with a workmate. I squeeze his shoulder, as he had mine, and give a long, roundabout, bilingual apology. Anouk's eyes communicate the same message but without the surplus. He shakes his head. "No," he says. "I'm sorry for *you*."

Anouk and I take a breather in our hotel room. She goes on her iPad to send a photo of the water park to her best friends. In the bathroom, I smudge my mascara just a little, to make it seem like I'd just replanted a plastic disc in my eye. I look in the mirror, at my raccoon eyes, and think, *Why play these charades?* They are time sucks, vortices. Some people are whirling masses of air. It doesn't mean that they are loveless creatures incapable of giving. But it does mean they're some kind of Bermuda Triangle at the ready to make you, or a part of you, vanish.

I hear the echo of FaceTime: It's Anouk's best friends asking for a virtual tour. I hear their giggles, then the sound of coqui entering our room through the parted balcony doors. "You hear that, guys? Hear it? That's Puerto Rico."

It's the mercy I need just as I'm sinking into a self-punitive mood. She might remember her grandfather's rudeness, but I have hope that the calming sounds and delicious air of this island will eclipse the memory, or memories, of it. That's the point, anyway, of this time-out in our room. Rest and recover. Emerge recouped. After her short call, we make our way back to the marina restaurant. I've wiped off my makeup, and on me is a clean, fresh face, a messy hair bun, and a clear head.

When we arrive, Stephen is alone at the table. And blissful. Two flimsy but still useful paper straws connect his lips to an abandoned Lamborghini. It's so big, it's like he's snorkeling. Before him is a king's feast. His arm brandishes, invites us to sit. It's gaudy; it's tacky. It matches his floral button-down. And I am here for the vibe. Just because, I curtsy. Anouk laughs. I don't have to ask Stephen what happened or where his parents have moped and limped to, if they're eating peanuts or club crackers from the minibar. They're not here, not where the playlist has circled back to the Dua Lipa we danced to earlier in the pool. Not here, not where I'm about to sink my teeth into an overflow of butter, bread, and lobster meat. Our very good team is very good at, and we've always known this, engorging. I want us to say *No more* to anything or anyone that encourages abstinence of any kind. Our desires: They shall not be extinguished.

Lips shiny from grease, I tell my loves, "Vacation should feel like dancing back to yourself, not running away from it."

They know what I mean. When the server asks if we'd like dessert, Stephen cues Anouk, and she says in a fancy tone, "Why, yes, one of everything, please."

Dispatches from Recovery

2023

I'm doing what I can to feel less alien. I want to feel less disconnected from the world. If I am, as they've all said, truly lucky to be here, then I want to feel that luck, that good fortune, that felicity. I'm almost a couple of weeks into brain surgery recovery, according to the dry-erase board on the wall, and it's been long enough to learn that no matter how kind everyone has been, no matter how many sweet messages and fruit baskets and floral arrangements people have sent, it is entirely up to me to get ahead or behind the two seconds that are either too late or too soon. It is up to me to drop the pin on the map of this existence, wherever it needs to be in order for me to not only feel like I'm not dead but also feel like I am still living.

What's felt good these past couple of weeks are the reciprocities likely negligible to everyone else but that have been every reason for me to dillydally here and not go and escape to the happy, painless, easeful places in my mind. It feels good to trade my hospital gossip (which nurse is sleeping with one of the residents) for Stephen's workplace drama (which teachers have made other teachers cry at departmental meetings, whose parent is dating the dean). It feels good to help Anouk with sixth-grade math. When Nurse Alexis comes with nighttime meds, it feels good to joke and call the large ones "horse pills" and make a whinnying sound that makes her laugh. When Nurse Mary Kate compliments my skin, whether or not she's lying to be nice, it feels good to not gatekeep the brand of face balm and serum I use. When Sammy's reliever, an older woman whose youngest turns sixteen soon, tells me she wishes she knew how to decorate a cake, it feels good to show her the website from where I learned a simple fondant technique. It's these times when a cherished book passage I read in my past life, something I might've dog-eared or copied down and has hence been cemented in the amygdala, fans out before my vantage and makes most things simple and clear. For example, one from James Baldwin to behold in these moments: "The longer I live, the more deeply I learn that love—whether we call it friendship or family or romance—is the work of mirroring and magnifying each other's light."

So when I learned that today is that most beloved and most problematic of American holidays, I used the phone that unlocks with my face to have a box of Thanksgiving-themed cookies delivered to the neuro floor. It feels good to open the box and tell the ultrasound technician or the radiologist or the resident physicians to "Please take one." And it feels even better when my two walk in with sweet potato casserole and sliced turkey, dressed like we're going to a rich great-aunt's or grand-uncle's, and I open the box to reveal that I've saved their favorites, the turmeric one and the one encrusted in nonpareils.

After they help me out of the hospital gown and into the cashmere sweater that brings back color to my graying cheeks, I sit and watch them ooh and aah at the floats parading across the television screen, something that's never been customary for us this time of year, and I welcome, even if just for this November, the grand marketing cavalcade. I press close into the moment, no matter how little I understand and no matter how unsure I am of today and tomorrow, and I lean into the possibility of tradition, or the possibility that ritual allows. I still don't believe in capital-T Thanksgiving, but right now it delights me to know that I'm not the only one on this planet with an ache costumed in festivity. The television is a box of silly little people with their pains and heartbreaks and physical conditions contained in silly little costumes or the best fur or faux fur they own. I'm sure of it—this is how most of us are getting by, and for having this to share, I am thankful. To show it, to own the ever-fleeting feeling of gratitude, I tell the girl to break me off a piece of her cookie. Treats held up, we toast to our oncoming sugar high. And no, I'm not recanting things I remember saying about this holiday and beliefs I've held fast to. I am, simply, mirroring and magnifying light and giving thanks.

8

Free Association

Spring 2022

The gift of home, of our home, is the gift of free association. Things happen and come to surface here; the biggest surprise is no surprise. At dinner, we hearken back to ourselves the thought that might have had the ignorance to slip, the idea that could have let itself drop through the metal slats underfoot through which the hot air burst from where the subway sped. We were just in Manhattan, a busy place, a happy place. In the city, we are never censored and are always inspired: by a fashion-school student clothed in last semester's final project, a magazine stand obsolete elsewhere, our beautiful, intelligent friends. New York was the overload we needed after a nearly two-year social and sensorial hiatus. It's its own kind of replenishing, but, because in free association we do not lie, it is no longer our speed. When the bags are somewhat unpacked and the heavier outerwear put away, it is time to sit around the table on the west side, the sunning-down side, of the ranch-style house and attend to the renegade thought or the backsliding idea, and to not so much discipline and align them but ask them to sit and cozy up. In the pink-orange sunlight filtering its way inside, there will be plenty of food for everything and everyone.

I'm stirring a pot of arroz con gandules while the tostones drain off excess oil. Recipes, I've decided, are my favorite kind of souvenir. I'm pleased with how I might have just now perfected the smash on the once-fried plantain. The second fry is so much cleaner, satisfying. Stephen's at the dining table, at the end of a Zoom call with his and Anouk's new Philippines-based Tagalog teacher. Anouk's posted across from him, sketching to ease off from these lessons she so detests. The first half of every hour-long call is hers, a half hour of picking at her fingers under the table. The formality of the lesson, the noun and verb agreement, the cognates and false cognates: They are not her style. To comfort herself from the fact that language learning is never easy, never truly compatible with anyone's ideals and expectations (unless, of course, you're a language nerd like Stephen), she impresses her volition upon a piece of printer paper by way of errant marks.

"Psst, Basquiat." I hold out a large medallion of twice-fried plantain. She sets her pencil down, walks over. I split the piece in half. We cheer. "It's hoo-hoo-ha-hot," I warn her. The plantains are really hot. "It's hard," I reassure her: language learning, coming back from a place that feels reciprocal and cogent, seeing your white dad adopt yet another tongue that should be yours. They're all really hard. She agrees but with an eye roll, so I don't know the appropriate follow-up. I hand her a stack of plates for setting on the table. She walks them over to where Stephen is and traps him between the Target wares. He's so cramped that he has to lift up the laptop, and this act of hers is petty and crude and poetic. She impresses me. He gets it. All she wants is to master this part of me, and all he wants is, well, the same.

His Zoom voice is a "cell-yell" and is loud as always, and I don't know why we're surprised that he's equally, excessively engaged as a learner as he is a teacher. "Should we give him an award already to shut him up?" I murmur, goofy and googly-eyed, to Anouk when she comes back to the kitchen for the guacamole.

When I've plated our all-starch meal, I approach the table that is now more tableau. He's an adored, haloed apple in a still life, aglow in the Zoom screen light and the doting of his teacher; she's a statue whose savvy is frozen in a balletic arabesque, her gaze a piercing scrutiny. I step into scene, a seer now part of the interactive art. Plates full and hot and heavy in my hands, I elbow Anouk's sketches off to the side so I can set down the viands. But just as I'm doing so, Stephen signs off the call in a way that he thinks will impress his teacher: a sentence lilting and dipping with pronouns and verbs in full Tagalog. What strings together in his brain at the moment is just past hilarious; it causes me to let go of the plates too fast and bang their ceramic bottoms on the table. I fall back into a chair before rolling off it and onto the floor.

"What? What?" he's asking.

For my child's satisfaction, I lag my response. I continue to roll side to side in laughter, my sleeves picking up dirt and lint.

The teacher is dumbfounded; she's quiet just before she lets out too many ums. My laughing takes over all the air space and saves her. She can hear me struggle for air as I laugh, and she, on the other side of the world and twelve hours ahead, is left with no other choice but to join me. It becomes a chorus of that high-pitched laugh that reminds us all who is who here. The teacher and I are both sighing at what we think is the end of it, but then we start again. It's another wave of overtaking comic relief. I feel like I'm having progressive, active labor contractions.

"Say it again!" I command.

"What? What did I just say?" Stephen begs for rescue.

He meant to ask her to join our meal, which is considered courteous in my culture. You never start a meal, not even a snack, without first offering it to others or inviting them to partake. He knew it would be rude to end the call and begin dinner without acknowledging the teacher. But instead of saying a rather formal "Would you like to join us in eating?" he says, with a wide toothy grin and cell-yell Ted Lasso voice, "I would like to eat you out."

The vulgarity goes over Anouk's head, thank goodness, but she's delighted to know that he's verifiably gotten something so terribly wrong, it has sent my body convulsing to the floor and my shriek of a laugh to the teacher's small village near an active volcano. Thanks to Stephen's overeagerness, I have sent maya birds flying across a rice paddy in a Philippine province I've yet to see. Anouk laughs the kind of near-soundless laugh that bubbles between your teeth, more inhale than exhale, and soon Stephen is doing the same but with his face in his hands. When he catches his breath, it's a curt "I'm sorry" before the laptop is folded down and slid away, and we begin our meal a clean canvas, ready for another round of agreement or disagreement and any and all ways we can say, "I'm glad I can be my pissy or obnoxious or trying-too-hard self here."

~

The stack of tostones dwindles. The tall glasses of ginger ale sweat. The cat perches by the rice, his whiskers tickled by steam, and we arrive at the topic of his first birthday fast approaching. How could it be? Our second pandemic pet is no longer a baby. From there it's a trellis of all things fast approaching, including Mother's Day and my birthday.

"What do you want, Mama?" Anouk asks.

What *do* I want?

Our constellation of wishes sets in closer; outside, stars prick through the new night. Around the table, it's swoosh after swoosh of gentle reveals. *This is it,* I think, *this is home: a place where a future flickers its blinkers, where we receive early projections shot from a later point on the tangled line of what we'll call, for now, "destiny."* Maybe I didn't want to come to America the way I did as a teen and maybe I still hold weighty grievances toward the adults who left me with not much of a choice, but when I had chances of leaving the United States with no guarantees of a legal return, when I could've just done it and left all its stars and stripes, a flash from a meal like this would dislodge me from what I then thought was my exit from here and my journey back to there. I would see hands not much smaller than mine, a girl miming my moods and movements. I would see his stubby fingers, nails bitten to nothing, on a keyboard, frantic in some search for some writing program or literary competition he's convinced is meant for me.

"I want to dye my hair ash-blond. Just for fun. Just to try something new," I say. I don't know what else the lighter hair color could represent from my future outside of, well, a feeling of being lighter. I show them a Pinterest board where I've been pinning images of summer hair trends.

We go on: more ways to try something new. A new sport that won't hurt her hip as much, like volleyball. A season of life past his once-groundbreaking, because his father disapproved of it, man bun. A vacation with my best friends, something we hardworking, determined immigrant daughters have never, ever done.

My latest pitch catches them off guard; I feel like a wacky contestant on *Shark Tank. But we're saving up for the Philippines,* the wry looks on their faces say. A long sip of my drink before I explain that I need another stop before we cross the Pacific. Puerto Rico is, technically, part of the United States, and I need a practice round with passports, customs, immigration officers.

"What do you have in mind?" Stephen asks, rubbing his palms together, interest piqued. He pulls his phone out, thumbs at the ready to swipe around for travel deals and paid tutoring gigs.

For more than a decade, Anouk has been my friend group's baby. I'm the only one to have had a child, and it's been sweet and fun and filled with outrageous presents from her aunties, all lavish as they're all vying for the title of "favorite tita," but . . . even Anouk is ready for someone else to be coddled. She's almost eleven. In a few months, another one of us former Upper West Side roommates is due to give birth to her Chinese Jamaican baby, and what could be a better reason to shut off our laptops, pack our bags, and share a kitchen and an itinerary? The starry night doesn't collapse on us or into itself. An admonition. It's time to plan a trip again but not quite yet.

Anouk's frustration with Tagalog lessons shoots back through the atmosphere like a comet no less obstinate than her, and it reminds me of where exactly I want to celebrate my thirty-sixth birthday: a restaurant close to the beach, aptly named for Charleston's ability to withstand hurricanes, Obstinate Daughter.

"Think for a minute, okay, then tell me what *exactly* is disappointing you," I say.

She's already thought it through: this just-unfolding internalized shame for not knowing how to speak her immigrant mother's tongue, something many diasporic sons and daughters carry on their shoulders. I tried to teach her when she was younger, meeting up at the library with my only Tagalog-speaking friend in the area at the time. She too had a daughter, two years Anouk's junior, still preverbal but already protesting by way of her scowls and toddling away to the DVD stacks as soon as a non-English word left our lips. Neither girls were hungry for it then, because why would they be? Their world was Mom, and she was all they needed. Mom was their consciousness, not motherland nor mother tongue. Her cradling arms and her soothing voice were already two big universes.

Anouk picks at her fingers under the table again, and the anxiety the habit suggests pulls me out of my travel and dining daydreams. I really don't care if she speaks, or even understands, Tagalog. She might be taunted for it sooner or later by the nativists in my family and outside it, but I really do not think less of her or think of her as less Filipino/a/x than me. I won't do in reverse and to the same effect what my girls-school classmate did to me. I will not shame. I will not bully.

"So what?" I tell her. We signed up for Tagalog lessons for fun, and to maybe help us prepare, in some practical way or some superstitious sense, for this mother of all trips to the Philippines. What's important is that we tried, together. "Hey, listen to me. So what." I tell her that kindness is our language. Laughter is our language. Water. Food. Magic. *Your heart. Pusong Pilipino*.

I assure her that girls who look "half" like her and stretch their vowels long like her and who've yet to see the sun rise or set over any of the seven thousand Philippine islands are just as Philippine as me if they receive and proclaim it. What makes her Filipino or Filipina or Filipinx is up to her and up to her making of it, and what matters more is what she does with the richness both the heritage *and* the history so offer. The preservation of a language and its continued use is, of course, important in the intergenerational transfer of a culture or tradition and of the preservation of a people's way of life, but to subject someone to shame is its own act of eradication, expunging. I will always choose to see my daughter fully as more than just a transmittal or medium. She is, I tell her tonight, not a vessel that carries nor a vessel to be filled. She is not hollow, not empty. I am a mother to her first. A Filipina second. A writer and teacher well past third. My job is to not load her with stuff, especially not if it might choke her. My love's work is to tease out the abundance that already resides within her since my and her father's twin stars collided and became one. Seeing and then helping her see this very plenitude that makes her links us in more bona fide ways to our precolonial roots than any kind of appraising or valuing.

"Oh, Bitty, what I love about watching you two do Tagalog lessons is not that you get the words right. Know what makes me smile? When you find very-you ways to remember a word, like the word for *white*, and you point at Dad and snicker, *Puti*!"

Just as I would never sacrifice the artist for the art, I don't place the language above the speaker. My child is a very compliant only child, a petite and brown-skinned Southeast Asian girl. She will be, for a good portion of her life, in spaces where she will be talked at, as opposed to talked to, where others will want to be near her for how they might benefit from her affect or presence or whatever it is that they might assign as a kind of deference. They will tell her she's nice, because she is, but also because they'll want to peg her as some model Brown child. They will be nice to her but for their own good and pleasure. They will either comment on how good her English is or how practiced she is in Tagalog, but both will be harmful flattery. Both will teach her to perform. This is why I don't subscribe to the philosophy of "You must be . . ." and instead hope and try to raise her in the truth of who she is: She is more than enough.

"Aunt Nancy doesn't speak Korean, but Uncle Jesse does. Do you think he's more Korean than her?"

Anouk shakes her head.

"Exactly."

Stephen begins to clear the table but makes a detour to the bottom drawer of the freezer. We almost always have ice cream (a pint of nondairy for me, the proudly Southern brand Blue Bell for them), or at least a small treat like a Twix. Dessert: another old-as-time and loving language.

"I miss them and New York already," Anouk murmurs.

"Yeah, me too. Why do you think we miss them so much?" It's a tool I've learned from teacher training. Instead of the instructor always spewing answers, have the learner speak it themselves. The aim is to foster the ABCs of student-centered education: autonomy, belonging, competence. Is that not what all humans want, immigrant or not? Is that not the point of language learning? To be yourself, to be of a community, to be trusted?

"Because with them"—she means Aunt Nancy who lets her pick out new outfits, Uncle Jesse who has the same obscure taste in music, and New York, where in every corner is another sanctification of not so much her individualism but of her essence—"we can be who we really are."

"Let's visit again soon?" I say, speaking it into reality.

Another New York trip, a possible visit to Jamaica, my return to the Philippines. These are precisely the kinds of plans we make and make believe in, that never make sense on paper or a digital budget spreadsheet, but somehow always, always, work out. This belief in things working out, it's something I'd like to think is more Filipino than ube ice cream. I've been a skeptic for much of my life in America, and it's time I relearned to believe.

PART III

PRACTICE RUN
Montego Bay, Jamaica

As was known to the Arawaks, Xaymaca, or "land of wood and water."

—November 2022

Dispatches from Recovery

2023

This cat, without a doubt, is my cat. And I am, without a doubt, his person. Cats don't lie. They don't sit on your chest or burrow in your hair after you've shown all your weaknesses—by which I mean being helped up two porch steps, which was after needing to be driven home, which was after needing to be wheeled to the hospital lobby, which was after crying when the last needle and tube were wiggled out from under my skin. When a cat sits on you after all this, you best believe it has answers for which you've pined. It likes you, not the hologram that you think you are. The cat whose face is so close to yours its whiskers are in your nostrils is a creature letting you know that you are home—whether it feels absolutely like it or not.

Sure, you're lying back on a mountain of pillows that smell like him and her; and sure, you aren't surprised by the creaking the bed makes when you roll too far left; and sure, you know how hard to press down on the dull buttons on the ceiling fan clicker. But when the cat takes a litter-box or kibble break and off your chest the fourteen big-boy pounds of him go, you feel less like co-owner of this house he and she have brought you home to and more like mismatched furniture within it. Your nowness and hereness are reactivated mostly by this feline's proximity; your feeling an impostor fades every time he climbs on you and purrs.

On your first night "home," a night he and she and you learn to describe as "harrowing," your body takes note that medicine is no longer intravenously supplied to curb the inflammation of your brain and spine. In response to the sudden withdrawal of pharmacological holy water, your body screams. It says, simultaneously, like a nation-state just post–civil war, Help! *and* Don't touch me! *He is trying to catch the pendulum of pain and stop it from swinging, and she is on the couch, pretending to sleep (so as not to be another worry), and whatever they do with the love and courage they still have for you—bring you ice, wrap you in your favorite sweater, oil you from temple to toe with lavender, distract you from the pain with schoolyard riddles—you say with your mumbles and every angry jerk of your body the phrase nobody really wants to hear nor answer:* Am I going to die? *If their willingness to vacillate with the waves of your pain and sense of self isn't proof enough that you are theirs and they are yours, then you can believe this: Out of obvious ideas but not of love and tender care, they retrieve the cat from the litter box or its feeding corner or the hammock it made in the tufting of your couch, and they bring it to you because it is language you remain fluent in.* Cat, *you understand now, means* sorry *and* love you *and* please let us help *and* we're trying *and* breathe *and* stay here with us *in every tongue you've ever spoken.*

9

In Jamaica No Strangers

Landscape here is a noun, and in it is me, the previously least photographed person in our family.

I complained in the summer that my image and likeness were elusive in my phone and Google Drive, and I appealed for someone—*anyone!*—to bridge the gap or stem the need because *I didn't take on sixty-two teaching and consulting projects this year to not be photographed in paradise.*

I was cranky. I was back, professionally and mentally, in that place where the more I told myself I needed to rest, the more work I took on so that I could afford to rest. I couldn't decide if I was being a good parent and good worker, as my relatives would praise and respect, or if I should've gone ahead and asked Urban Outfitters to make a graphic tee mocking me: Internalized Capitalism Baby. I was starting to feel in the small of my back a shooting pain that would not abate, like the chaos of my never-ending columns of profits and losses. *It'll be worth it,* I kept telling myself, adding another row to the spreadsheet and imagining the kayak rental or lobster roll the gig would pay for. While each addition proved that I could turn a good profit as a full-time freelancer, a reality I was willing to test with vehemence at my lowest in my NGO job, I had not found the formula for work-life balance. I did and do, however, remember what my peri- and postnatal yoga teacher used to say when it was time for an inversion or one-legged stance: *Balance is not stillness but a negotiation between opposing motions.*

Feeling in the yoga studio then the opposing forces of my long-held ambition to write and my overcoming desire to be a good mother, I tried out her theory and learned to introduce writing to motherhood and motherhood to writing. I welcomed the pull between what I had been conditioned to think were East and West and was rewarded with an opportunity to fix my gaze and my wonder at the open space breaching between. What I saw in the lists of tasks, the calendars scribbled all over, and the tax forms claiming refunds for both a dependent and freelance business expenses was a palindrome: something that read backward as it did forward. Motherhood fed my writing and brought to it an urgent but caring perspective; writing (and reading) fashioned an original out of what could have been a weak shadow of my mother's quintessence. I have never done everything right in these twin literary and parenting pursuits, but I can, with a philosophy born out of an asana, say that I've always done it my way when I could have believed that there was no way. A friend once told me, sincerely and without resentment, "I wish I were self-actualized like you." I think it's this bicycle motion she was referring to.

On a day like today, when a morning shower relents to striking sun, there's a rainbow connecting what was then and what is now, and capturing it in high definition through a plane window is the almost-eleven-year-old to whom I've lost access to my phone. She calls the rainbow a "lucky coinkydink," and the water beneath it a "crystal blue," and these may be the last verbal markers of a childhood, the last hurrah of what even a still or moving image could not do justice. She is, after all, wearing something salvaged from my Goodwill pile: a boxy yellow number that of late was looking like a too-short tent on me and is now looking like an intentionally, perfectly oversized pullover on her.

We are, I tell my best friends, in that era.

I was lucky that my flare-up last summer was concurrent with Anouk's new hobby, that my wishes for proof of a lived life came as she was signing up for the middle school photography club. With her mother nearing middle age and volunteering (forcing) herself as subject and providing through this series of travels depth upon depth of field and a range of motifs and locations, she has my phone and its charger attached to her still-tilted but healing hip. To prepare for what is a joint birthday (hers), baby shower (my friend Brianne's), Thanksgiving, and World Cup trip, we asked for Polaroid film from grandparents and at-home mobility exercises from the physical therapist. Both will build a kind of strength, I thought, and there was my adopted theory on balance again: go and see, see and go. Feet on the pedals.

When we deboard, we remember that the late-pandemic travel surge delayed our trip by a day, booting us off one flight after the other and branching our course, ultimately, toward a sleepless night in the most clamorous corner of Fort Lauderdale, Florida. The airline-provided hotel was not only next to a railroad but also only within Uber Eats delivery distance of a very short list of restaurants. Pollo Tropical was a franchise name familiar from our time in Puerto Rico, and so from there we ordered. To my distress, the brown delivery bag contained fewer items than ordered and paid for. A side that *was* delivered, I would learn soon enough, was the one that poisoned me: a paper bowl of spoiled beans. The air conditioner growled all night, thank God, as it muted the growls I was producing in my time of crisis. When I emerged from the bathroom for the fourth, and hopefully last, time, Anouk and Stephen joked, "Want us to take your picture now?"

I was too weak to be clever or pissed, and I collapsed on the bed, next to the suitcase that, by the way, was stained all over with facial serum from an apothecary bottle that, like me, apparently doesn't travel well. Cold-hot and sweaty was how I entered the night, and this morning I came out of it hot-cold and parched. Desperate as I was delirious, I challenged fate, screaming, "Nothing will stop me from Jamaica-ing!" Reluctant traveler no more, I overcorrected. Learning, as they say, is a process.

Almost twenty-four hours since we left the bunny and the cat with my cousin, and here I am, held up by three ginger ales sloshing in my system and using every ounce of energy to make myself look not sick, not like I could be suspected for having COVID, and escorted by an airport concierge recommended by Brianne and whom Stephen had the courage and presence of mind to book online and splurge our gig money on. For a military brat conditioned to never order drinks or appetizers when eating out, this is character-building stuff. *It'll be worth it,* the soothsaying chant goes.

The concierge and his lanyard become our beeline past the snaking, ambling queue to the health pass and immigration desks. If I weren't regaining strength after our Uber Eats fail, and if standing in line didn't cause Anouk pain, this VIP treatment would feel too prim: a complete one-eighty, as the movies say, from my typically curious, arduous experiences that involve IDs and forms of any kind. When our passports are stamped, I squeal (squeak) to the best of my abilities, because not only have we officially and smoothly been welcomed to Jamaica but also it is our family's first shared passport stamp. Stephen high-fives us, the fanny pack slung at his chest emphasizing how much of a sitcom dad he really can be. He's here to announce his happiness and his being a tourist, and it's sweet because it's genuine. A man who knows gratitude? A true provocateur.

The concierge then leads us to a lounge where I deflate as soon as I enter. When Stephen walks off to investigate where he can withdraw cash for tips, I crumple into a felted chair, and I am offered an herbaceous and floral drink I learn is made of sorrel: a hibiscus variety. I take it as a sign. My first book has a hibiscus on the cover. The juice is the color you'd expect from punch, pink where the ice floats and red where base, sugar, and spirit mix. As soon as I bring it to my lips, I feel my queasiness return. One sip and I'm sure: It's an alcoholic laxative, not juice. I set it down.

It's the Mexico versus Poland match on mute on the lounge televisions, and I can feel the concierge taking the room's temperature. Can he watch the game? Can he stand closer to me, where the view of the screens is unobstructed? I ask him whom he's rooting for, which team is made for the Qatari desert heat. He sidles up for more of my sporty banter and to see the screens better. I almost ask him to sit but don't. I don't want anyone getting in trouble.

He asks Anouk, who is munching on plantain chips, "What about you, eh?"

The dimple that appears next to his grin shows that he's impressed with how she can, in her shy but heedful way, talk sports with an adult she's only just met. She says she's for Mexico, mostly because of her proximal knowledge of the language and culture. "But then," she also murmurs, "many of the Polish have had to leave home too." Heartened by these acknowledgments, he's now got the polymer tray clipped between his arm and side, hands free to do most of the talking, fingers mimicking plays. Her eyes follow his imaginary football headlong for the goal, but before his imaginary striker makes the shot, our shuttle driver's calling to tell him that he's waiting at pickup.

Stephen meets us by our luggage, a wad of small bills puffing up his fanny pack. The concierge escorts us once again. And again, I don't know how to behave in this conga line of preapproved privileges. I hide my face behind sunglasses, only to realize that it all but enhances the finicky nature of the whole ordeal. I really have no interest in keeping up with a Kardashian, Kim or otherwise. I just want to have fun without aggravating any one person or any one culture. I fidget with my purse, pretend to be looking for something while walking, as the self-conscious do in their cars at a traffic light, on the bus, or at the bar while waiting for a date. It's so hard to accept the good when it's been withheld many times, many ways. These comings and goings are, if you aren't coy to call it, so hard as well because we all still live in the long shadow of colonialism. There's no fixture or fitting that doesn't feel awkward, no mechanics that don't feel like a cog. By design, colonialism did not have people like me or my friends Brianne, Buki, and Nancy in mind. We're all women of color and immigrants or daughters of immigrants, no matter our education or accolades or jobs. No matter our "no accent." Life is most consistently capricious; we are kept on our toes. They might say we are welcome to travel and leisure, but implicit is the invented order that having to be invited or be welcomed or be told upholds.

Travel exposes not just this pit, but who cares to see and avow it—and who doesn't. Most of us on that plane earlier today are suspect. But not all of us plead guilty. "What is a journey for? To remember, to forget," said the essayist Anna Badkhen. It cost us one hundred American dollars to have this concierge service and to quicken the process out of the airport and into the chirrup of Montego Bay's savvy streets.

Twenty years ago, I arrived at SFO as an unaccompanied (unescorted) minor. With exactly one crisp Benjamin that my sister's best friend tucked in my knockoff Tommy Hilfiger at the Manila airport, I was then already much richer than a majority of three hundred million people currently in diaspora, twenty-seven million of them refugees. But it still felt like not enough of an asset. I held on to that bill like it was my life, scarcity becoming the defining feature of my existence. I learned to hoard not merely things but representations of security: coupons, jobs, connections to jobs, and pennies saved for a down payment and a belief in home ownership that when fulfilled felt like a mountaintop religious experience. Inevitably, like a mountaintop religious experience, it is followed by a descent of some kind.

The value of one hundred dollars, or at least the constant consideration of it, followed me through my late teens and early adulthood of cleaning houses, waiting tables, and nannying. There was a swap at some point, the old Benjamin for a new one. What was consistent was my fear of not having *at least* two zeros following a one when I checked my bank account or looked in my wallet. One-zero-zero will always feel like a million to me. As well, it will always feel like it amounts to nothing. Even now, when I buy a week's worth of groceries for our family, I watch how close I can get the tally to that baseline. The farther it wanders away from 1-0-0, the more anxious I get. When I buy groceries online, I am constantly deleting items from my cart. In person, I am always putting back an item before weaving through the final aisle and to the cashier. It's rare that our weekly groceries as a family of three humans and two pets is ever right at one hundred, but the gratification I feel when I skim back toward it or only hover right above is perhaps as close as I'll ever get to the experience, or illusion, or delusion, of conquest.

Our shuttle driver Mike was also referred by Brianne, who is now nearly two years into her reverse migration from New York to her beloved Jamaica. Promoted during the pandemic, her two decades of no stopping finally afforded her a chance to answer the call of home. Able to wager her experience, tenure, and loyalty to the company, she worked remotely and returned to the place of her girlhood and began claiming for herself all things formerly evasive: a nurturing relationship; a young Jamaican motherhood surrounded by elders, sisters, and other supportive and helpful company; and morning coffee and afternoon tea by a bay. Her return, like a woman-reaches-middle-age movie, inspired me. Looking at her photos on Instagram, I felt I too could be brave. Like her and like the third of American millennials who boomeranged during COVID, I too could go home. But at my will.

But not yet.

Stone by stone, I lay a path. I already have the nurturing relationship, and next on the docket is the kind of motherhood Brianne now enjoys, one surrounded by supportive company. I have wanted this since March 2020, since the world shut down and life closed us in. As Mike weaves us through Montego Bay, past handicraft markets and a Hard Rock Cafe, around a cape buoying a hulking inflatable slide and down a single-lane road, I feel the gentle but energizing pull of sisterly love. Stephen rides shotgun, already in a groove with Mike and having made him laugh, already having explained how we know Brianne.

"They're the famous Eighty-Third Street and Amsterdam girls," he says to Mike, like Mike should know the meaning of the cross streets.

"Famous?!" Mike looks at me in the rearview mirror, looks for my face behind my prescription sunglasses.

"Yep. Big-city girls making their way home."

Mike simpers, "Ah, yes, I know what you mean, man."

He drops us off at our Airbnb at a condominium with a resort-style pool, and Anouk is befuddled once again. And once again, she is monosyllabic as she was in Puerto Rico: *Ma! Mom! Look!*

I'm rifling through Stephen's wad of bills for Mike's tip, and I give him more than half the stash. Stephen glowers as if to ask what the heck I'm doing. I pull my suitcase up to the curb as I hand him what's left, telling him, "We have American money we can always earn back. You have more than a hundred dollars in the bank?"

He nods.

"Then you're rich. You have equity?"

He nods again.

"That's more than what most people have." I tell him he can find an ATM again and hope that he remembers that despite his teacher wages, by simply being a white male and having a salary just slightly higher than our country's median income, he is already better off than 90 percent of all of history.

He says nothing else and pulls his lower lip over his teeth, like he does when he knows I'm right about the baby's fever or the intermittent whir in the dishwasher or the important letter in the mail that he mistook for junk. A man who can also admit fault? So incendiary.

"Ma! Ma! Look!" Anouk's louder now. I think she's calling to make me look at some lizard on a wall or through a breezeway to the ocean, but I'm mistaken. When I turn to see what she's calling my attention to, it is the sightliest of sights: my dearest friend Buki, in her floor-length wraparound and red-orange lipstick nonetheless. She's radiant, my Nigerian queen. She glides, because she does, and I pull to her. I'm reminded that she salvages secondhand wedding dresses and restores them, handwashing and re-hemming them until they are elegant and pure as ever. She gives sheaths and pleats and lace overlays a second life, returning them to their former glory.

We meet under the reception awning and hug.

"You're here. You're finally here," she says, squeezing me tight as she always does. Our ribs touch. "What do you think, eh?"

Already in step, already in context, every sentence between us feels mid-conversation. This is how it's always been, how it will always be, no matter how long we have between these familiar hugs. She's asking what I think of Jamaica, how it looks, how it *feels*, to *me.*

"Well." A pause. I take off my sunglasses to reveal a smize. "I think all recovering nations feel the same."

Her perfect, pearly teeth beam through the red orange of her lips, and it's the same smile she wore when she watched us exchange vows at Central Park and the same smile she welcomed baby Anouk with into the sisterhood. She takes my luggage from me, takes Anouk's, wiggles off our hands when we sort of resist, all the while maintaining the sweetness of her tone and her face, and says, "I know, eh. I know what you mean."

Outsiders on the inside.

Hands free of her purple suitcase, Anouk grabs my phone from my hand. "Ma! Auntie Buki!" She snaps a shot, a perfectly angled palm frond just behind us to create the illusion of depth. But there is no illusion here, not really. When you're in a place where the motto is "In Jamaica no strangers" and you're in the orbit of someone who too has left and searched for home, vacation is no mirage. There are no tricks. It isn't a fool's paradise. Friendship is landscape, a noun. A place, a richness to recede into. Scarcity is the illusion here. Lack is not the language.

Dispatches from Recovery

2023

"Faster! Push faster!" I yell through the mat of hair and snot on my face. "Baby kitty! Where are you? Baby!"

The louder my yell, the stronger the pressure on the nerves on my neck and face, the tighter the crimp on the rupture site and the bigger the throb on my forehead, and the sharper the pinch on my spine. The thing is, although I feel all this and feel loud, I am not loud at all. My whole body screams, and the sleeping squirrels and neighborhood children remain undisturbed. I say again, "Faster! Push faster!"

"I'm trying, Mama," the girl says, out of breath and willing for energy she doesn't have, shouldn't have, not weeks into helping to care for me and attending to her studies without my support and answering every "How's your mom?" thrown her way. She pushes. She pleads, "Call louder, Mama. He only comes to you."

"Ba-by! Come to Mama!" I exert every painful syllable out of me, peeing myself a little in the wheelchair, sobbing, begging the god of the universe to give me, us, a damn break. When you've lost parts of your brain and your sense of self and any bit of equilibrium and the ability to hold yourself up and steady your feet or control your pelvic floor, the last straw life can pull from you is the cat who makes you feel more like a living thing and less like a coatrack. "Ba-by! Ba-by!" I cry to the tempo of the girl's urging us forward. I feel like a shapeless

gathering of dirt in a wheelbarrow too heavy for her. But she pushes with all the frustration and hidden anger of a quiet, obliging, loving girl who almost lost, or is slowly losing, her mom and who might now lose her cat on the eve of her twelfth birthday.

In the dark of the dead end of our street, under the cover of hundred-year-old oaks and drop curtains of spindly Spanish moss, a shriek finds us. The girl pilots the wheelchair in a U-turn so sharp and quick, I nearly fall forward. She pushes me toward the sound we didn't know our kitty-kitty could make. We arrive where our recycling bins face our neighbors' and find our big boy cowered and shrunken in the middle of a feral cat circle, tail puffy but ears down, a sign of his imminent surrender. Just before this suspected acquiesce, the girl jumps into the circle and disperses the ferals, with only a Target-brand sweater to protect her should the freaks attack. She's so big, *I think, but then I look again with hopes that there's nothing to worry about, nothing to worry about, and in just a blink or two, I see that she's not at all big, never has been—the reason we sometimes playfully call her Bitty. I see that she's become who I used to be before the aneurysm. I see the resemblance now. She's not at all big but is enshrouded by unruly hair I haven't brushed in too long and by the puffed-upness humans make when they're full of fright and have no way of showing it beside feigning size or strength, cosplaying greatness, and pretending to be exactly what a situation needs them to be.*

10

Circumnavigation

The other motto for the trip, it seems, is "Try and try and try and try."

Setting precedent with my spoiled-bean misadventure, the group transforms into a control room, the rental becoming a central operations space for tackling disasters. In the three-bedroom condo with a Wi-Fi connection we are quickly overwhelming, Buki, her also-puti husband Kyle, Stephen, and I stand in a trade war with the Airbnb host. *We'll deep clean before we leave! We will be quiet, a group of mostly introverts! We are good people! Compliant!* At the risk of stereotyping or tokenizing ourselves, we keep throwing promises and any and all negotiation tactics we've collectively garnered in our careers in education, healthcare, and freelance writing. We are people who've haggled in our day jobs, with middle schoolers and patients and publishers and their respective middlemen: parents, general practitioners, agents. And so here we are, hopeful only as much as we are, I hate to say it, useful. What's a male nurse, a good Nigerian daughter, a Filipina former nanny and cleaning lady, and a Southern military brat supposed to do?

We have overlooked the finest of prints, it seems: too many adults for the listing, per post-Commonwealth rental rules. Enough sleeping space for eight but only four adults are allowed, and we wouldn't have to be in such a dilemma if I, a former legal reader and NGO fact-checker and current developmental editor, hadn't missed that caveat to another caveat. I try to fend off the lie that the minute I am lax, the world falls apart. *Hiccups are a part of travel,* I think to myself.

While I ask Stephen to ask Buki to ask Brianne to ask her husband, Brandon, to ask his friend who has a friend who lives in the same building to petition for our case, I task Anouk with figuring out how to get the World Cup on any of the three televisions. Her one-girl operation isn't as successful as our multiform strategy, but when she acts all unbothered, I remember that this is a vacation, not a fight. There's no need for a trauma response or a mission strategy. I'm not on high alert for an early weekend morning call from my former boss at the NGO, and we are not deploying photojournalists and reporters to an earthquake zone or refugee settlement. The missed detail is just a little crease we can smooth out with the back of our moisturized, sunscreened hands. Kyle hands me a sorrel beer, and my stomach now settled, I take it—because not only "in Jamaica no strangers," but it's five o'clock at some sticky airport bar somewhere. I say cheers to the travelers still stranded and waiting to board or waiting to make the call to call it quits.

Nancy and Jesse are on their second boardable flight, but on a higher-level count it's their fourth airline booking, and it's already a miracle they'll make it here also only a day late, given the international travel delays in these late-pandemic times. If we hope, if we make believe, if we really want to test this whole "we deserve good things" theory, we can ask the gods and the ancestors and the clovers and the birds: Just one more miracle, please?

They take heed. Brandon's friend's friend pulls through. The building manager calls the Airbnb host and green-lights our group of six adults and one child. The reason for the exception: We are not strangers. We're here to visit a homegrown beauty and her new baby girl, our suitcases packed to the brim with pom-poms and baby aviators and crinkly sensorial toys screenprinted with Someone in South Carolina loves me. We're not here to get wasted, although we're not judging people who've come for that.

We're here for reasons far less bombastic and far more, how should I say, low-key: to reunite around a kitchen island after pandemic isolation and to shower (more like sprinkle, really) Brianne with much belated congratulatory love. *So they're family* is how matters are settled. And because of it, in one fell swoop, trust is built and formalities are swept under. The conversations move from the limiting Airbnb app to the emoji-filled WhatsApp, and Nancy's and Jesse's names are added to the guest ledger downstairs. Mike swings back around to the rental compound and accompanies Kyle and Stephen to the supermarket.

"The one with the ATM, OK?" is my directive.

From there, the two buy sundries for the next few days: fruit, wine, cheese, and more cheese. They buy cake. Not long after Mike brings them back to the Airbnb do we get the call from Nancy. They're here. It's time to, in our own idling, subdued but not snoozy way, party.

Looking back now, I understand that beginning in my childhood, I rarely found time or reason to be happy because I was too busy being strong. Nearing my forties now, I've never been more resolute about anything than my mission to reverse the fact. I entered motherhood so young, at barely twenty-four, and I used to be filled with such a regret and self-doubt that ate at me. How dumb and irresponsible, I secretly thought of myself and my decisions. As I sit here, I am overcome with retroactive excitement: I entered motherhood so early and doing so gave me an earlier motive for, and more time to, experiment with this thing called happiness.

In Jamaica, on our last night together, Buki asked what my hope was for midlife. I told her I wanted to enjoy life, to rest so good that I face the world the next day ready for my most loving work, at home and in the world of words. She gave me her blessing by taking a photo of me in my mumu at that moment, reclined in a corner cushion of the sectional. "Hold it," she said, maybe referring to my pursuit of happiness. "It's a beauty."

Dispatches from Recovery

2023

You ever write your name too many times and start questioning how it's spelled? You ever look at the spelling and wonder how a selection and arrangement of symbols, some other someone's invention, come to mean your person? Your shape and the very space you take up on this planet? Your worth? And then after all that, that name could grow and compound even more in meaning, by an addition of some prefix or suffix (like, Anoukie) or the subtraction of a syllable (Nouk) or the curling up of an end sound or the doubling of a rhyme (Noukienouks). It turns out, when you've lost your sense of self because a blood vessel erupted in your skull and blood ate and rearranged your brain's parts, spelling your own name is the least helpful thing you can do (and one of the first things they'll have you perform at the ICU). When you're healing from all that and regaining what you feel belongs to you, the best course of action is to let your web of friends and family catch you and to entrust them with the big (and somehow, yes, thrilling) and oft-exhausting task of search and rescue.

We humans, at least the last time I checked, can't grow more limbs. Nor can we say to our existing ones, Stretch out—c'mon, we need length here. *But our brains, I'm learning from both my neurosurgeon and Doc TikTok, can regenerate and build new or reconstruct broken pathways, and while this fact isn't really secret, key to the wonder of human physiology and biology is our capacity (and primal need) to relate. The weeks my two best friends visited and played the role of home-health aides were perhaps the weeks when the most and speediest retrieval took place. This is not to offend nor to discount my two. This is to say that a grown woman with a spouse and a child, both her most-prized in this existence, still very much needs her friends. Just like a teen scoring close to 1600 on her SATs who got her driver's permit on the first try might still need her bunny or teddy, an author-editor with a mortgage and no cavities and whose CV is as long as her last CVS receipt might still need her Nancy to say, "Uh, yes, we're the same," and her Buki to call her by the sweetest of pet names: Cinelle-Belle.*

I wish I could formulate it for you, what they did. But when I was being patched and sewn together by, coincidentally, two earthlings I met on New York's Fashion Avenue, I was too preoccupied with being reborn in this girliest and womanist of ways. They brought me my favorite moisturizer and rice-water facial cleanser. They brushed my hair. When Stephen was on the phone (for hours, I kid you not) with our insurance provider, they spent the same amount of time showing me photos of me and of us from years past, like they do with slideshows at people's memorials, only this was a coming-to-life. They said that although I'm short, I had limbs for days. For days! I began noticing then that I had an elegance—and an awkwardness. Nancy kept me company by listening to all my woes (mostly about my lost income and if I'll ever write again—or even want to). She refilled my tea. She also unboxed and trimmed the reusable snow-white tree we pull out every year for the holidays, and she made sure to spice it up with Auntie Energy by gifting Anouk the year's first new trinket: a needlepoint and half-naked Harry Styles. Plus, she made sure to station me and my wheelchair where my shoulders squared the spectacle, with the box of ornaments (each one a soft punch of sentimental value, many of which brought home from Disney World, Puerto Rico, Jamaica, or the Philippines) secured and open in my lap.

As for Buki, her magic wand just as godmotherly, filling my pantry with packets and cans and my freezer with two-step meals was her way of kick-starting the one activity, apart from writing, that made me feel like myself. The woman was poising me to cook again. "Semi-homemade meals to warm the house and thaw whatever this recovery time had frozen," she said. Sure, there were tears. Women cry to each other. But there were even more laughs, which hurt my healing spine like a cruel brain freeze that moved down the lumbar. We laughed at Nancy's uselessness when it came to nurse duties. I peed my pants twice while she was here because she couldn't figure out how to get me to the toilet. Every morning, Buki emerged from the guest bedroom burritoed in all the blankets we owned, her slim Nigerian body never acclimating to the humid, clammy and yet cold, subtropical Atlantic-blown Charleston winter air.

There were also many ho-hum moments when nothing was notable apart from the fact that we'd grayed at the hairline together. We were once just girls, once just students, once (nervous) debit card users, and now we have credit! They entrust us with jobs, children, and loans! By the time Nancy and Buki left, winter had gone deeper into itself, and it was easier to be sad than to fight it. And even then, I was thankful. Much of my semblance had returned. I was again vain and whiny and judgmental and argumentative to extents my people and I could forgive and embrace. Their spoonful of gossip helped the medicine go down. I could again thwack a joke at the dinner table. By the last meal we shared before their departure, I could again make my best friends laugh by picking on me and Stephen, how incongruous his Southerness is with my immigrant city-schoolness. And how our incompatibilities were just right in amount and nature, how they made for us a magnetic field strong enough to keep me on this earth. Same old jokes, same old rhyme. Same old warm feeling you get sitting around with humans who've known you since the first time your debit card got declined (and they said, "I got it."). Same not-so-old humans who've every power to salvage your eccentricities, normalities, and sundries.

By the time Nancy and Buki left, it no longer bothered me to look at the spelling of my name. After all, it's just letters. I am more than a symbol of myself. I could cosplay Madonna, Gaga, Bader Ginsburg, or Sailor Moon, and there and then I am still an amalgam of everything I do and don't remember. What matters more, what gives me my strength and stead, are the people willing to play house for as long as I need them to, that I may again feel at home in these four walls and in these for-days limbs and rice-water skin.

11

Echoes on a Windy Cape

Everyone's always talking about a mother's love. But what about a daughter's? A daughter learns her mother's ways, trusting fully, at least up until a time, that this mastery would bring not only the world but peace with it. A child's learning is their way of love. Like she drank from my bosom, a fact I will and can never claim to be a fruit of my laboring or thinking, mine now imbibes at what's become, because of the physical closeness and logistic entwining the pandemic has caused, the open bar of my existence. She takes it all: the brio, the (often sudden) lack thereof, the renewal of such, the cause or motivation for which. She copies how I comb my hair, then proclaims it is the only way to do it right: whiff out the knots at the ends first, then stroke all the way down from the scalp. She knows too every soon-forgotten category by which I organize the pantry. She'll tell her dad, moving what he's just unboxed and put away: "Dad. Peanuts here; pretzels there."

Accustomed to my falling in and out of health kicks, in and out of a love of kale, she nibbles around the hard, bitter stems, saying, "Not bad." What she doesn't say, because a daughter's love, at least now, at least hers, is magnanimous: *Not good.*

I used to be negligible, forgotten. Left alone to raise herself in a house caving in on itself, I was the child who made new toys out of old ones, who went to the seventh-grade dance in her brother's polo shirt and her mother's awkwardly big bangles. I was the schoolkid the nicer schoolkids were extra nicer to because at the end of the week, I smelled a little. We did not have running water at home.

For lunch and dinner money, I turned in Coke bottles at the recycling kiosk near school. I didn't know what a fruit was. It was always canned meat from a sari-sari or skewered and grilled innards from a street food stand. My big brother, when he liked me, stole candy from a magazine stand or gas station for me. "Here," he'd say as he chucked the Bazooka Joe or Pop Rocks at me, turning around so quickly, I never knew if he wanted to be thanked. Stolen candy: the only way I was looked after.

When I think back to all that now, my thoughts will sometimes correct themselves. Maybe it wasn't that my parents forgot about me but remembered me, wherever the hell they were, for all the wrong reasons and in all the wrong ways: the clever kid, the kid who can do. *Oh her? She'll be fine. Thank God. She's my smart one. My good one.*

Then I was "relinquished," a word I equally associate with my teen adoptee self and with anything that starts off exciting and after a time becomes, because of this "relinquishing," sheepish: a once-amiable dog, a once-ferocious cat, a former talker in class and at Mass, who, after her immigration and adoption, turned into the Brown girl who supped her strawberry Yoplait and apple-cinnamon Nutri-Grain lunch like a toothless baby, as quietly as she possibly could, between the least visited stacks in the library at the predominantly white school. Now you see why the brio and the often sudden lack of it. Why the kindness, then the cutting tone. I am ups and downs but no longer impossible heights and depths, thanks to the self-love and the love and expertise of others, and borrowed money and the time and resources it afforded, that have altogether moved me through the stages of trauma recovery. Meeting Stephen at age twenty was meeting kindness in the flesh, and seeing him cry of pride and happiness and a healthy fear of responsibility at Anouk's birth is the most cliché and most true example from my life of what it means for someone to commit to providing safety and stability. He was Stage One.

In the throes of early motherhood, when I started to believe that the incessant crying I was producing was more than the regular baby blues, I consulted first with a lactation support nurse and then a licensed trauma specialist about how a familiar but heavier feeling of worry had burrowed so deep in my marrow, my arms would sometimes be too heavy and unable to hold the baby up to my breast for her feeding. This happened. And I really did say this.

I was textbook, as they say. A childhood trauma survivor who had coped for so long by dissociating and compartmentalizing and by doing the kind of doing that makes you forget (*So hardworking!*), and then: motherhood, the portal, the amorphous but not shiftless force that breaks the levee keeping out the tide. Stephen and the trauma specialist were in consensus: To move forward, I first had to go backward.

I had to do the work of remembering, of returning. I got to it by writing bit by bit, on index cards, every time I sat down to nurse the baby. Ten to twenty minutes each time, six to eight times a day. The more I nursed and the more I wrote, the more sore my nipples got and the lighter and stronger my arms became, and the higher I held up little Anouk to my chest. The more I wrote, the closer she was to my physical heart. They say an infant is nearsighted, only seeing up to their caregiver's face when held at the chest. Beady eyes, taking me in. The easiest of any mother's tasks is to look at her child's happiness. The hardest of our duties, if we're survivors of childhood trauma, is to keep staring into that happiness and believing it will stay.

The more I gave, the tougher the pink-brown skin on my nipples became. I was feeding, no longer leaking. I was also being fed: The more I wrote, the more of the residue of my childhood suffering I offset—displaced—out of me and onto the page. That is to say, the more I gave, the more symbiotic it became. I was given back space within myself. I stopped crying from all the hurting. By the time she was toddling but still nursing, I had three shoebox containers of these index cards, of these stories from another life and time, like little brittle coffins; I had something physical to look at and mourn. I had no intention then of making public the story of my childhood; it was a private exercise of processing and remembering and creating distinction between what was and what no longer was. By putting into words the "it" that had burrowed in my marrow, I unburrowed it and gave it another place to thrash or wallow or die. To continue into its death. This is what the textbooks call Stage Two.

On the heels of these two stages came two nonfiction books. I was no longer just "writer" but, as once-peripheral people who'd sidled up closer and closer had started addressing me as, "published author," like I was to be proud only of the product and not the process. The concept of "success" and "deserving it" diluted the whole of what I'd attained: meaning. The act of publishing became secondarily traumatizing in this sense (extractive, like colonialism and its cousin, capitalism, are extractive). As well, by the nature of the publishing trade, I was, once again, destabilized, unstable. Waiting for paying gigs (not just gigs for "exposure") was a replay of looking for Coke bottles under gym bleachers and between parked cars. I still didn't eat fruit. It was as though I was still getting rewarded with canned meat. I still had to hold on to the ones and the double zeros. The general attitude was that you lucked upon these paying jobs like they were Coke bottles, lucky you, and if you dared stop looking, well, *you should be grateful.*

On one hand, it was not new. People had been talking at me for as long as I could remember.

So cute.

Give her the world.

On the other hand, it was a distinct kind of, here's that word again, *exposure.* The same uncle who quips at us about how simultaneously wondrous and unsmart it is to live in a place like Charleston once sat next to me at a funeral so he could whisper, "I see you have hundreds of five-star reviews online. Does it pay?"

I did not answer.

What I've learned from twenty years in America is that you can be grateful for, and still be shaken by, a reality. Of course, it's a rare and therefore privileged experience to write about your childhood and hear yourself and others call it "art." It's a truth and a twin to another truth. Writing and publishing my debut memoir also became a source of much crippling anxiety that would lead to my having an anxiety attack while on a book tour. And as had been modeled for me or as my parents showed me their way of reckoning with hardship, the way out was quite literally that: to leave. I left publishing and applied for the one and only job I could find in our part of South Carolina at an NGO that had use for my journalism degree, writing and editing skills, and experience with traumas and disasters of all kinds. *Perfect for the job,* they called me. I didn't yet know that I was merely swapping one exploitative experience for another. I would be poisoned yet again with the concept of "doing good for others, no matter what." In less than two years of working eight-to-six, plus weeknights, weekends, and some holidays, I was out again and into, if I wasn't going to throw away what I had sowed and reaped previously, Stage Three. It's that time when a trauma survivor has cycled in and out of forms of therapy and, finally, applied what they've learned. Mainly, for me, it was to believe and then live out the truth that I was worthy of the reality I was determined to achieve. That it was right for me to want. That by wanting, I was not stealing candy from anyone. Nor did anyone have to steal for me.

That I didn't always have to be the smart one, the good one.

I quit the NGO job and the nonprofit industrial complex. I sought publishing and consulting work that paid, negotiated my terms, and asked for what I was due. It was groundbreaking, for me, to ask for fruit and not canned meat. I taught memoir and essay writing classes online, mostly to writers of color, so I could walk them as far as I'd walked myself: far and deep into a creative practice that not only stretched my mental muscles but engendered self-empathy, self-empowerment, and joy. We were building for us a new environment, since all trauma and therefore all healing was and is environmental, relational. I began to believe that I could have an existence beyond survival. That in the right company, I'd thrive. That I could leave the work of Empire for the nourishment of Ecosystem.

I became a balayage blonde, then a brunette, then a blonde again. I grew my hair out. I learned to crab. I took up space. I said to myself: *Wish you were here.*

I said no when it didn't immediately feel like a yes in my gut. I started divesting my time and energy from predominantly white work and social spaces. I got a passport. I used it. I gave my daughter something other than "hard work" to drink. I lived out my modes outside productivity mode. I lived the story I wanted to tell: This is a story about an immigrant woman who, like nature ought to, revived, restored, rewilded, returned.

I organized the pantry. And I didn't.

I organized my books by genre, then color. A rainbow for a wall. *Ma! Look!*

I relearned volleyball so I could teach Anouk, then I tore my shoulder. I learned to hit with my left. I was bad, then I got good, then I was bad again. It was fun.

We went to the mountains, and I took a nap. When I awoke, I met a horse named Poet. His brother's name was Prophet, and his sister's, Throttle. Kind aliens, gentle giants. They looked like us, their large equine eyes like a mirror in front of a mirror: endless images. We learned that riding a horse was about learning trust: the giving and receiving of it. When we rode them through the brush and streams and fog of western North Carolina, the earth mossy and slippery under their hooves, it was the first time I knew what it meant to have safety and security while not needing or having control.

I tried to eat kale. *We* tried to eat kale. The bunny loved our leftovers.

Not bad. Not good.

So what?

We stocked the fridge with Blue Bell and nondairy ice cream. We stopped fitting into our prepandemic jeans.

We needed new clothes. We made new ones out of old ones.

Anouk wore my bangles, and they looked right.

She wore my tops, and they looked better on her.

"You look so much like her," Buki says to me now, at the kitchen island in this shared kitchen at the Airbnb I've decorated with crepe paper pom-poms in Montego Bay. "I mean, you do. You look just like her. Uncanny, uncanny, uncanny." She says it three times, incantatory.

Notice who she says looks like whom.

There's a cake, a store-bought vanilla and chocolate one. There's white frosting slapped on, an artificial blue airbrushed in an indecisive cursive to say Happy Birthday. It looks homemade. It looks just right. They have their phone cameras at the ready. "One . . . two . . . thr—"

Stephen, then Kyle, rifles through the cupboards and drawers. There is cake and there are candles, but there are no matches at the Airbnb. Stephen runs downstairs to ask the building manager for a lighter. Nancy is impatient and wants to already photograph her goddaughter. She rifles through her purse, as if she smoked, as if she owned a lighter. Buki is more impatient. She so badly wants to celebrate this human that I happen to look like, to sing already.

"We can make . . . a fire," Buki, the schoolteacher, declares, and I immediately protest. She's already sticking a rolled-up receipt in the toaster when I begin to remind her that the reason why we all scattered away from the apartment on Eighty-Third Street was because we had a building fire.

Smoke slithers up from the toaster.

"Buki. No."

Her kaftan sleeves sway with her movements and come too close for my comfort to the hot metal appliance.

"Have you lost your mind?" I yell, covering my eyes. "I am not a part of this!"

Nancy, the most stringent and the oldest and most self-made moneyed of us, sighs, "Fine." Orphaned so soon, she does not typically toy with danger. She's the rare New Yorker who waits to cross the street or avenue, the fashion executive who still hand-selects every material, still assists in the making of patterns and cutting of fabrics. Nancy is the designated guardian on my will and my insurance policy. That is, my most trusted. She rolls an even thicker wad of paper towels into a miniature cane, a makeshift torch, and sticks it in the toaster. I feel betrayed.

"NAN-cy," I hiss.

She ignores me, and I feel the irk from every time she waited too long to, or never did, respond to a text message from me. Work has had a chokehold on her for as long as I can remember. But friends are the occasional deserters you pursue, the occasional traitors you keep. These particular friends descended from different wars but inherited the same tired and tiring work ethic, the same filial piety that has bound us to over-committing to employers and jobs. To the imagined ascent promised by the manufactured American Dream. In a way, we were raised to be traitors to ourselves. Maybe it's not so wrong now to want to start a fire. Okay, okay. Maybe this I can forgive.

"Another rule, Bitty," I say to Anouk, who is still waiting by her cake and watching us argue, "is no sticking things in the toaster, okay?" I tuck a piece of hair behind her ear, and she lets me. But she neither agrees nor disagrees. She twists her lips, like she's thinking. Her aunties clap their hands at an orange flicker. She looks away from me. A cheery bumbling rises at the arsonists' end of the kitchen, where all the outlets are. Their little win starts to feel offensive, and I shake my head and ball my fist in my pocket, but none of it drives me to need to fashion a vacation within this vacation.

Buki's plan is a bust. Nancy's support of it amounts to nothing but a new gray hair at my temple. All they produce is smoke and more smoke. I take a pom-pom from the mantel and fan the smoke out the balcony door with it. My *r*'s trill: "This is so, so irresponsible, you guys! We're gonna get in trouble!"

Notice: It's not the fire nor the danger of it that scares me. It's the thought of getting in trouble. It's the fear of getting caught that keeps me from letting out a laugh.

Kyle and Jesse back up to the wall and watch. This is how they support us: by letting our friendship roil, as it sometimes does.

"You don't know. You don't know if he found a lighter," Nancy whispers, turning back the other way to study the width of her new torch. "We have to sing 'Happy Birthday.'"

"Yeah. Yeah!" Buki's words are punctuated by a kitchen drawer slamming back in. She won't give up. She's looking for more things to stick in the toaster. The way she's biting her lower lip says she's determined. "Last time we did this, she was two, man." She's referring to when I was still on the fringes of postpartum depression, no longer forlorn but could, with any burdensome task, like a kid's birthday party, turn into a hot plate on a slow burn. My friends flew to Charleston from everywhere to pipe cookies, hang streamers, and, yes, stick candles in a cake. They caught me in their arms as I crumpled into a broken origami bird in my kitchen, overwhelmed not so much by a party but by the reality of parenting when I, myself, had not been parented. I had crumpled to the floor because a batch of cookies came out burned and because the antidote I've learned to use against the lack of safety and stability I'd grown up with was to get things right the first time, all the time. Buki said to me then, while unfolding me back into an upright and fleshed-out form of a woman, "So what?"

"The only way to survive is by taking care of each other," said the activist, author, and philosopher Grace Lee Boggs. While she was talking about the beauty and power of mutual aid and Global Majority solidarity, I apply the wisdom here, in the mutual sense that each of us has healed and can't help but want healing for others, and each of us has come in the others' aid in times of unemployment, postpartum depression, a mother's death from cancer, the onus of wedding planning. My friends are, like my Stephen and my Anouk, more than proof—evidence!—that nobody heals or journeys home alone.

Sometimes, in the maturity of a friendship that has withstood a prewar building fire, a pandemic, our scattering throughout the world, countless jobs and their determining economies, and the long shadow of imperialism, care is the very recklessness that love and its actors introduce to your life. It's the opportunity for a laugh, the invitation to the elements to spark something in the toaster. Around a rented and shared kitchen island on a windy cape on Montego Bay, care might just be allowing yourself and your friends the kind of abandon that your white counterparts have in the summer movies, in the beach reads, in yogurt commercials.

I give recklessness a go. A lifelong insistence on being and doing right does, eventually, come to be its own grief. It's a grief that feels like a house suddenly bigger, longer, with floors suddenly deeper, after all the lights go out at the break of thunder. You feel displaced, misplaced. Like you could, at any moment, fall. I motion toward the toaster and on the way grab the paper towel cardboard roll lying on the counter. The rub of naked cardboard in my hand in itself already feels like a little fire. My nostrils flare; baby hairs stand around my ears. I should really trust my friends more.

I'm about to stick the cardboard in the toaster, my other hand turning up the dial for more heat, when Stephen walks in, his signature grin plastered across his face and a yellow Bic lighter waved by his ear.

"Y'all. I asked someone, who asked someone, who asked someone . . ." He goes on and on, recounting the short story–like search for a lighter, the dips and turns and peaks, all evidence of his incomprehensible patience. I can bet that none of it upset him. I personally would have given up. He keeps going, about fire escapes and almost twisting an ankle, until: "Hennyway. We got us a lighter, y'all."

He takes the breath he hasn't taken since he walked back in here. We all laugh. Kyle extends a congratulatory handshake. On his way around the kitchen island, I hug Stephen's side because he has not only kept me from creating the next arson but also kept the candle-blowing dream alive. Thumb on the small, scratchy lighter wheel, he sparks a flame and lights the candles. His crow's feet deepen as he smiles. "Ready, Bitty?" he asks our girl. He's the patient dad he never had, the venturing father who ultimately returns to his daughter with a promise fulfilled, and who, for myself, I am still waiting for.

Jesse dims the recessed lighting. Our faces glow orange around this happiest and most semi-homemade of birthday cakes. We sing, at varying tempos, because even the most universal song is sung differently in different locales, by different peoples. Anouk's striped shirt looks holographic in the low and peachy light, and when she sways to our singing, she seems to come forth and back, forth and back, the dancing optics of a child being sung into the breaking moments of her twelfth year around the sun.

My daughter's love is her learning, and here she is receiving all that my dearest friends, her father, and I have to offer. How lucky are we to be trusted. We are examples of hard work at the office and on the therapist's couch and examples of standing up for truth and justice and sitting in the cozy of joy and love. We are also each an experiment at deserving better, which could mean, like tonight, opportunities to fail, to be ungrateful, to be audacious enough to stick things in a tricky appliance and maybe get kicked out of an Airbnb and to call it all a sacrificial act. To call it a comedy. To not expect reproof. To do unquantifiable things, like finally eat my very first strawberry. Buki and Nancy not long ago bought for me my very first strawberry from a farmers' market, and in the safety of their nonjudgment and the invitation, but not pressure, to partake, I sunk my big beaver teeth into what tasted and felt like a sweet, spritzy, herby pink mallow. I know a fruit now.

Carl Jung said, "The greatest burden a child must bear is the unlived life of its parents." The family I've made, the friends encircling me, the travels we've made believe and made happen have altogether left only a few stones unturned. There are more experiences to be had, surely—more candles to add to the lineup each year. But there is no unlived life of mine groveling in some corner for lack of attention. There is no self left in exile.

When I try to remember the moment in the bathtub just two years ago, I'll sometimes hear Anouk's baby-er voice say something about seeing the world. But I'll lean into the memory closer and hear, clearly, echoey as conversations are in baths, that she said she wanted to see *my* world.

A cruise pulls into the cape, smaller and quieter than I'm used to in Charleston. Exterior lights go out one by one, like before a concert; smaller, flickier, interior lights turn on. The cruise and its people hover on the water like a city. The water carries over to us sounds from the floating metropolis's outdoor disco, and Stephen jokes to Anouk, "Surprise! We ordered you a party!"

Gone are the days of crying over burned cookies. (I was the burned cookie.) My new gift to my daughter is this self-redemptive way of life, born despite the brutality of how intergenerational trauma and colonialism and racism and capitalism and perpetual servitude conspire to make us hate ourselves.

The ship's acoustics continue to boom in, bass on bass. Glass and metal decor clink to the beat. Strobes dart into the dim of the rental apartment and replace the glow of the now-blown-out candles. Jesse takes photos of us with a film camera, while Nancy captures the ship's reflection on the water. In months' time, they'll be photos we hang on our refrigerator.

Echoes, echoes.

Kyle pops a bottle. Champagne bubbles are exactly how I feel.

Stephen circles Buki, who is circling Stephen. They are, like their eccentric, innate ability to give and receive, a koi fish dance.

Mid–viral TikTok choreo with Anouk, she stops and turns her shoulders to square mine, her hologram of a shirt swishing to a halt just before she throws both arms around my neck. She stands on tiptoe, and our eyes become level. She says, bringing her foggy breath up close to my ear, each syllable sticking to the vanilla icing on her teeth just before they go and go and join the wind, "Thank you, Mama, for everything."

Dispatches from Recovery

2024

Now here is where my friends differed:

While rubbing coconut oil into the mat of hair on the back of my head, Nancy offered what she said was a way out. The house I worked so hard to own, she said, was sitting on too much coveted land. The excess, she believed, must be put to use in a way that will alleviate my profits and losses sheet of too many writing, editing, and teaching commitments. Build a rental, she said. Take a break from publishing. She reminded me of the hazards of my job: too little security, too many ways to get the writing wrong, too many rounds of working and reworking that surely, now especially, isn't good for a healing brain. These are all good reasons to step away from something that exhausts emotional, cognitive, and, sometimes, physical reserves. I had never taken her for superstitious, but in that moment she said, coming to the end of detangling my hair, "And you were writing when the aneurysm ruptured!"

Buki, on the other hand, said the opposite, not through words but actions. Unpacking brown bags of groceries, she pulled out a five-dollar word search booklet and a pack of highlighters she later left on my nightstand. She asked me for book recommendations, mostly to elicit the kind of excitement she knew I've always felt whenever I got the chance to rave about a book or an up-and-coming talent in one of my classes. After dinner one night, before the dining table was even cleared of plates, she propped open her laptop and asked me to dictate a thank-you letter to everyone who had helped our family through the difficult recovery season. Once it was all typed up, she said, "An essay! We wrote an essay!" And from that announcement I borrowed what I didn't yet know was my superpower. We *just wrote an essay, just as* we *just decorated the Christmas tree, just as* we *made it to every travel destination I promised* we *would visit, just as* we *got me to the ER, to the ICU, to the operating table.*

And because both Nancy's and Buki's offers were irresistible, I called a draw between them, and, as I am coming to feel has always been true to who I am, I didn't choose one over the other but instead treated both like pedals attached to the same forward-moving wheel. I've resolved to take one as a means to the other: My way out is some form of assistance from others. My exit will not be from writing but from the solitary way I've authored a life in letters. As soon as that resolution was made, a truth echoed from some recess in my brain, some pocket in time. Loud and clear it went: We have a good team.

12

Within Walking Distance

Life is veering. I can feel it.

We walk in a comfortable silence, our easy forward movement just a kind of relenting to the Airbnb's promise of access to a semiprivate beach. If we could, if we forgot that we were in the Caribbean, we'd stay in the apartment and close the blinds and lay our heads back down where we left the sweat of sleep to dry. We would nap. This absence of talk is proof that there is a need for a nap, but it would be completely negligent, if not disrespectful, of us to forgo our only Montego Bay beach day. It's a short Thanksgiving trip. Besides, there's no forgetting you're in the Caribbean in Jamaica, not when the palm fronds tattoo their shadows on the exteriors of homes and across the width of right-hand-drive streets.

It is also imperative that I use this brand-new and bright-red donut floatie I lugged through three airports and many detours, and that, still deflated and tucked into a square, took up half my carry-on. I feel like this overpacked carry-on now. *We* all feel like this overpacked carry-on now. Our big breakfast of garlic rice, chopped tomatoes, runny eggs, rum cake, and birthday cake has caught up with us, and whatever energy we woke up with was spent drinking beer-tumbler-sized mimosas and watching the Germany versus

Japan World Cup match. It's very becoming, being slowed down like this. It looks good on us, like our range of burnt sienna to vermilion swimsuits looks good on us. When the adults have forgotten every and all agendas, the one child in our care can, as she wills, stop to pick up fallen bougainvillea petals or turn around to crow back at the rooster taunting us from his perch outside a residential gate. *What have we done,* is what I keep thinking, *that a quiet walk like this has come to yet again feel out of the ordinary?*

I am happy watching these fools trip on their flip-flops, or say, "I'm okay," when someone offers to take the beach bag or the cooler digging into their shoulders or hands. If this is it, if this is the whole of the getaway, I'd take it and go home fulfilled. This walk feels like one of our easy Saturday mornings spent meandering down from Eighty-Third Street to gelato on Seventy-Sixth or to the farmers' market on Seventy-Second. We'd bumble out of the building and spill onto the sidewalk and sidestep stacks of Manhattan garbage, singing SWV or Aaliyah, twenty-three-dollars rich altogether, and happy. I remember thinking while running out of the burning building in my underwear at three o'clock that muggy July morning that life's cruelty just wouldn't abate, would it? For all that we'd survived, we had to add a building fire too? To the Brits coming? To Japan's invasion? To tribal wars and to the premature death of parents? To being uprooted and losing citizenship in your teens? To the incorporation and exploitation of our talents and gumption?

Finding each other at fashion school was the rekindling of the idea of home and of family for all of us, and when our apartment was snuffed out in the middle of the night by a downstairs restaurant's kitchen fire, it was like we lost home and family all over again. New York: birthplace of many chosen families, of secret sororities. After the fire, the morning walks together are what I miss most. Sixteen years since, we've carved out lives, again and again, and today's replay of those long-gone Saturday jaunts through the neighborhood, when New York still had neighborhoods, feels like a kind of unexpected recompense. And because this might be the last year we call ourselves young, even if our faces will inevitably continue to conceal our ages, onward we go, grateful that our achier, knobbier knees keep supporting us in our taking steps together. We walk. We keep walking.

When we've slalomed the half mile, or in this realm, the nine hundred meters, to the semiprivate beach, the words *temperament* and *proper* and *rational* fall out of our heads, and we are, like babies in utero, in nirvana, untouched by the worries of the world, and our only know-how and want-to is to float. The sea is the kind of blue that every millionaire's pool aspires to be, and its layers slide underneath each other, like manta rays cutting into each other's space, fooling us to expect a kind of crash when what they ultimately give us is a glorious, sparkling dance. There's movement but no waves, no sound, and I don't think I've ever heard a silence like this. For a former talker in class and at Mass who became the high school mom and who came of age in a hamster wheel, most kinds of stillness have come to scare me. But this, this is a happy silence. Behind my Kardashian glasses, I am in tears.

I run. And I never run. I board my floatie. I kick off. The invisible manta rays move with me. A nature scene like this will move you, and I mean *physically* move you. In front of my child and my love and my friends, I've just performed a miracle of kinesis. I make believers out of them, and they approach the sea and touch their toes to the hem of the water in an effort to catch me and my impressively large and unapologetically red floatie.

They try. But the water has taken me and I'm already far away, so they squat to the sand wherever they are and watch me float. I'm adrift in their gentle gaze. After a while of watching me hang in the calm tide, they get to doing their own thing. Nancy finds seashells. Anouk and Buki stir the sand with ticklish feet, and I hear them giggle from the kissy-kiss of minnows. Kyle swims, head under. Jesse uses up a roll of film. And when I look over, all of them in miniature, Stephen is still standing with his hand curled at the forehead like a visor and his toes to the edge of the sea, his grin and chin identifiable even from where

I am, his strikingly pale skin a flashing sign, a flare, a tall landmark, like a lighthouse, for me to paddle back to when I'm ready, his loving-kindness blowing over to where I am. I smile back. I tilt my head and lift a finger, a love-you and hello. He grins bigger.

I look at all of them and think, *What a story to tell.* Next door from this half square mile of semiprivate beach is Secrets Resort. We are separated from the honeymooners and lovers and retirees, who are mostly white, by a drop net and red-and-white buoy markers and a budget. But we're under the same sun and in the same water, all the same. Secrets, all right. A feisty thought shoots through and I want to wade over and ask them, *Have you ever heard of such a happy immigrant story, one that has nothing to do with being saved, doing right, or earning our way? Have you ever heard an immigrant story where there isn't much of a plot and the only action is lying in the sun and tumbling in the shallows?*

But I also wonder to them in my mind: *What are* your *secrets? What lack or sadness brought you here? What might you be recovering from?* Travel possibilities are as endless as the reasons for them: miscarriages, divorce, a suicide in the family, the ten-year death anniversary of a daughter, cancer coming back. These are reasons for travel that friends and family in the South, in the Northeast, and in Europe have shared with me. Often, travel is a soft launch into the other side of a very particular grief, a specific loss. We lose ourselves to jobs, to partners who hurt us, to abusive places where we once sought safety and were falsely promised comfort, to perimenopause and menopause, to a loved one's advancing into dementia, to a child's birth that forever changes our circumstances, to a child conceived and yet never born . . . There are endless kinds of grief that prompt our travels, that make us check the savings account, and withdraw from it what might become, hopefully, a redirection back to a familiar, comforting time or a familiar, comfortable self. So, yes, I feel pride for how much money I'm saving compared to the people at Secrets, but I also feel, if these reasons do apply, a sincere but short-lived sorrow. I kick the water at my feet.

My floatie circles back to shore, and my girl pounces as soon as I'm close enough to flip over. She's successful. Hair thick with wet sand, nostrils aflare from the attack of salt water, I accept the invitation to wrestle, burning my skin on the floatie's plastic every time I hitch up my thighs. I grunt and grunt, my movements no longer a miracle but a show that could make other, more proper mothers wince. But she is so strong, able to push me off as soon as a considerable amount of my mass is hiked up onto the inflatable. She's laughing and I join her, because it is funny, to have come to the point of your life when you, even when you try not to, move like an old stick shift.

"Ah, excuse me, ladies," someone says. It's a man, louder and closer now, a local in a fitted lifeguard shirt, looking like some kind of official. "American?"

I nod, even though I'm unsure what "American" means here, in this moment. I say, "Is everything okay?"

"Jellyfish, ladies." He walks knee-deep into the water, and from where I earlier imagined manta rays dancing, he scoops up just to the top of the water a translucent blob pulsing in slime. It's an alien disguised as a fine crystal dinner plate, gorgeous as it is gruesome.

And of course Anouk asks, "Can I touch it?"

"Gentle," the lifeguard says. "Tide bringin' 'em in, eh. Moon jellies. No-fear, no-fear. No-sting. No-fear," he says, as if two words brought together by a hyphen make the statements more true.

Jellies have, like me, floated their way around to shore. I hear our group approach, a radius of curiosity circling in around this man who took it upon himself to tell us to have no fear.

The lifeguard returns to his post on the posh side of the cape, looking out for more people to offer his anti-warning to.

Here between the blue of the cloudless sky and of the dancing water, another returning is happening. I feel myself split. I go back to the first time I met each one of these people currently knee-deep in the water with me.

I'm at a college hall.

A dormitory.

I'm on a rooftop in New York City.

A Long Island beach crowded with spring breakers kicking sand onto my blanket.

In the warm, slippery, bloody soak of a birthing pool.

A breakfast nook covered in takeout boxes in DC.

The juncture of these separate, although nothing in time is truly separate, memories: the absence of fear. I have been met with the message many times before. I remember now. And this re-membering, this suturing, this was the veering I was feeling on the walk here. Miles to meters, left-hand to right-hand drive. It's the perfect topsy-turvy to encounter anew a comforting kindness that has traveled with me through time, and that like the alien jellyfish camouflaged in invisibility, I only later realized has been there all along. It's not that there is actually nothing to fear. The absence of fear does not equate to the absence of threats structural, interpersonal, psychic, or otherwise. The absence of fear in the company of my dearest friends is the presence of something far deeper than cellular, far more mysterious and knowing than the cosmos. My people call it, I remember now, *loob* or *kalooban*. An inner self. And alive in that inner self is *dama*, a sensitivity to the inner selves of others. Beside the Tommy Hilfiger knockoffs and the worn Tretorn sneakers, loob and dama are what I brought with me across the Pacific to SFO on March 8, 2003.

At the college hall, at the dormitory, on the rooftop, on the beach, in the birthing pool, at the breakfast nook: the self in me saw the self in them and said, like the chorus of acolytes and nuns at my childhood Catholic school used to sing, like the young devotee in me used to sing, "It is well with my soul."

Being undocumented meant I had no valid IDs, no proof of a natural-born or naturalized right to stay and live in the United States. There was no Social Security number assigned to me, my movements, and my whereabouts. I had no credit score angling me for worse or for better, to ups or to downs, for hard lefts or slight rights. I was nowhere, it might have seemed.

I was floating much like an invisible jellyfish, drifting from cool to tepid to warm waters, coming so close to people who'd needed hearing the phrase: *no fear*. It didn't always work. Many didn't believe. I was adrift but not held in someone's gentle gaze. Even when I had gained citizenship and all the right papers, many, like the two cashiers at Harris Teeter and Stephen's grandmother who believed he was marrying Danger herself, only saw in me a lack, which they interpreted as a threat. The mind sees what it wants to see, doesn't it? A healthy dose of fear in our nervous systems keeps us safe; an entire worldview of it is just ignorance. The self in me fails to see the self in you.

But my dearests, they saw in me what I saw in them. Mirrors staring down mirrors. Spirit renewing spirit. It was interpersonal, intercultural, interstellar competence all at once.

Buki calls to us for a group photo. "Quick!" she says, her pointer finger on the timer button on her phone. Anouk and I hoist up. We all gather and bunch in close, the sea behind us. We have a water bottle for a tripod, and it tips back just when the proverbial shutter clicks and a mattress of a cloud rolls in above us, cooling the tops of our heads, and what we get is a souvenir photo not quite ideal but that none of us hate.

On our walk back, I whisper to Nancy that I've just received a travel writing assignment from another dream magazine. Her response is a wide smile and raised, excited brows, and they mean everything. Ahead of us, under the bright but yellow-mellow Jamaican sun, the rest of them walk with wet flip-flops, a paste of dirt and broken leaves crusting over their reddening heels. Their cover-ups move like capes, billowing back. Superheroes in plain sight. Their power is that rare thing that is softness. Their gift to me is trust. I trail behind them, catching headwind bits of songs that Buki and Jesse are surprised Anouk knows the words to. Aaliyah. SWV. Newer ones too, like Helado Negro and SZA.

"We are," I tell my best friends, "in that era."

Dispatches from Recovery

2024

How can anyone do this? How can I ever measure up to who she was? A house, a family, three books, and another one on the way? I have to finish her work? I have to write a travel essay and complete a book? How? You know, I'm proud of her. I admire her. I love what she's done to the house, with her wardrobe, the potted flowering plants in the yard. But let's keep it that way. My anger for her wakes me up at night; let's not drag it into the daytime too. I want to be her, and that feels impossible. The hole she left behind feels too big. I'd fall right through if I stepped in. Here, here is good. The chair I sit in seven hours a day, from when he and she leave for work and school until they arrive home and help me up and to another part of the house. The chair from where I do word search puzzles and work on coloring books all day. Easy, attainable, rehabilitative tasks. But finishing her book? Writing her essay? That's exactly what I mean by dragging my anger into the daytime. I can barely read a chapter of her manuscript before triggering a headache. When the pain and fatigue are overwhelming, I have a hard time recalling names for things and I stutter—oh, do I stutter, especially at night. There are times when I reach for words—reach, reach—and they never come. Why is that? Where have the words gone? One night, I was trying to explain to Stephen that I needed to eat dinner early because I could feel how empty my stomach was, but I couldn't remember the word you add before another word to emphasize its meaning. The word was very, *and I kept reaching for it and it wouldn't come to me and I got mad and started slashing the marker on my dry-erase board like a knife: V HUNGRY! V HUNGRY!! And he pulled up a footrest to sit on, and he quietly fed me my dinner, and I chewed and felt like a crazy idiot. I'm starting to feel at home here with her and her dad. But I picked up that manuscript, the one that had yellowed on the kitchen island, and I read it, and it took me weeks to do so and people kept saying, "You'll do great!" and "You'll get better in no time!" But it's almost spring, and I feel like we've gone so far forward only to step back again.*

13

Adventure Awaits

"You still got good form, Mama!" Anouk yells. *Still got, good form.* Words meant to encourage me twofold: that I am *still* alive, that my body still knows the language of survival. I've been teaching people how to swim since I was eight or nine, when I taught my childhood best friend how to dog-paddle in post-mudslide floodwaters. I've since taught a niece, a neighbor's son, another neighbor's daughter, and her, the daughter hurling my way what to her are lifesaving, secondarily traumatic words. I don't want to fail her now, not when I've bragged for so long that she's a good swimmer because I'm a good swimmer and because my own mother swam competitively. This is the daughter for whom I entered this lagoon. I was the phone and Polaroid safekeeper, but Neyo, our young and energetic tour guide who is lightning made flesh, said, taking the devices from me, "Hafta show your daughter you're brave, ma'am."

One minute I was blowing bubbles through my teeth, mouth wide and jaw soft. The next minute my biceps and triceps and glutes and hamstrings were learning just how much stronger this waterfall was than all my major muscles combined. My torn shoulder remembered it hadn't completely healed. The ache in the small of my back turned into a Bermuda Triangle, sucking into it my dwindling stamina and confidence.

Everyone was laughing not too long ago, assuming my flailing was some sort of joke. I was laughing too. I remember it, along with so many suddenly urgent things: where I am, where I am from, where I hope to be, and who I hope to be there with. But when you're preserving life, what you're really preserving is energy, so while moments from recent and not-so-recent times and my heart's humblest and loftiest desires flash before me, as the tabloids and self-help books say they would at such a moment, I attend to the water thrashing at and matting the hair on my head, and I part it with my freestyle arms and hands.

You still got good form, Mama!

How does she always know to say the right words?

It is not my time. *Not today, Satan,* I say in my mind, in my best impression and bastardization of Stephen's proselytizing ancestors. I need to needle through this water and rocket forth, or it takes me. I will my arms and hands to do better: candlestick fingers jetting into the water; webbed, amphibious fingers pushing water back. I keep my perfect form despite how tired I am, telling myself to be as thin as a pencil, as precise as a seabird in its diving pursuit of fish.

But I remain stationary, like an LA girl during her morning swim in an infinity pool. I am frozen in time and place, no matter how much and how hard I move. No matter how much I give. I wonder what Stephen's seeing. Porcelain gleaming in the water or his wife struggling? I hope the former. I don't want him to jump in. There can't be two of us here for her to watch and remember like this. I send him a message through the water and up the rocks: *Do not jump. Stay frozen.*

My vision remains blurry. I can only make out what's within arm's length. And right there, beneath me, up to where my hand can reach and where the aqua and cyan blend and separate from thrashing white water, my child self appears. She's the girl with beaver teeth who taught her best friend how to paddle to land and who raised herself in a haunted mansion crumbling into rich, anguished, long-suffering volcanic soil.

How serene she looks, with her hair long and flowy and prepubescent body not too scrawny despite being underfed, and it's exactly how I've hoped to always know and remember her. Our eyes smile at each other. Then her lips part, a bubble forming at an open mouth and ballooning to where my head dips under the water's surface, lending me air. She's aiding me like I've aided others, showing up like my two have shown up, just like that, out of nowhere or from left of field. She begins to speak. She says, assuredly, in our language, "Go stealth."

Magic words spoken, I float face down and unmoving, limbs lifeless, chin touching chest, looking like I've lost. I stir a silent, breathless panic among my people and others standing at the rocks. What I'm really doing is collecting force, my child self tells me. *Stop moving. It's okay.*

Later, when I'm splayed and catching my breath on the rocks, I'll think of how simultaneously fighting against the turbo of a waterfall and getting caught in a state of being frozen felt like being undocumented all over again and how resting, to no one's surprise but mine, saved me. I'll understand that the same was true for my nephew, my oldest sister's son. He'd started showing physical signs of burnout the last time I visited and watched him come home from his New York finance job, and as shocking as it was to find out he'd soon quit and pack up and go home to the Philippines, it was also no surprise he'd finally done it: upped and left and replanted somewhere beachy and that felt, down to his bones, like home.

In the beginning of his reverse migration, I outwardly displayed judgment, saying, "Who just says 'Fuck it' like that?" But deep down, all I had was big auntie pride and massive millennial envy. I showed Nancy and Buki a photo of my nephew in his new seaside home and sustainable life in Palawan, and Nancy's first response was, making me really question this lackadaisical version of her, "He's even more handsome now."

I clicked my tongue at her. I was trying to make (fake) a point: You don't just stop—not, especially, if you're an immigrant daughter or son. And *she should know this*, was what I was thinking, again my judgment rising fast from my abdomen. For a seer, my gaze can be so hot. There are times when the cruelty I'd absorbed from the world blurs my vision. So I am compelled to ask: *Had I missed the memo?* Are we all just, just, just giving up now? By *we*, I mean any human being who's survived an immigrant or military or traumatic childhood. I thought, *So much for being told to be strong and resilient.* What about "What doesn't kill you makes you stronger" and "Good job, my good and faithful servant?" Were these not the refrains that gave cadence to our mostly undersupervised latchkey-kid days? We were the kids who had to grow up overnight, who entered the workforce with "real-life" skills demanded of nobody but the most depleted of us, and I'm the one now acting surprised by my nephew's "sudden" exit when, perhaps, it was premeditated long before the world taunted with words like "quiet quitting." And did I not, although in a slightly different fashion, make my own exit from the NGO? And before that, from publishing? What if *quitting* and *exit* aren't quite the right words because there is no ultimate dream or routine or lifestyle or setup or trajectory to step out of or abandon but only an ultimate and sole commitment to ourselves, which is to say, to our constant reinvention? To how time plays tricks, how our outlooks change, how we are each many people?

Nancy took the phone from me so she could zoom into my nephew's photo and say, in a breathy, desirous voice, "He looks happy." She's on a plane back to New York now, and I wonder if her forehead is to the window and if she's still lustful over this newfound happiness of his.

"Ma'am, ma'am, you're brave, ma'am," Neyo says as he places the safety rope in my hand. He dove in and torpedoed to where the water was calm, just half a meter down from where the rapid waters slapped at my floating body, and swam under me to pull me like a rescue submarine.

For effect, and to console everyone watching, I kicked my feet just enough while he pulled me, a pantomime to say that while I momentarily stopped moving, I never stopped breathing. Now, rope in hand, I use energy I've regained and pull myself to the muddy embankment less than ten meters away. With Neyo guiding, I urge myself sidelong to land, already feeling a release in my back because I'm not swimming head-on against the current. Lateral's the way to go. It all seems obvious now, but that's the way it is. We and our better options are, even with contact lenses in place, the least glaring things to ourselves.

When my and Neyo's knees have clambered out of the water and landed on moss and dirt, Neyo says again, "You're brave, ma'am."

"Pfft, for almost dying?" I say out of the corner of my mouth, turned away from him to fix my swimsuit, pushing into it whatever needs pushing back in.

Unaffected by my show of self-pity, he's already pulling himself up by a low-hanging branch. "You're brave, ma'am, for trying again. Here. Allspice. Chew."

From the branch, he plucks a leaf and tears it, half of which he reaches back toward me with the expectation that I as well have propped up to my feet. He pops his half of the leaf into his mouth; I do the same with my half and gnaw like he gnaws. A potpourri of cinnamon, clove, and pepper blooms around my taste buds. Through the calming tingle coating my tongue, I say, "Trying what again?"

He doesn't respond and just moves fast. He's back to being lightning made flesh. When he charges up a narrow and slippery trail, his strides long and his knees hiking up, I have to follow closely as if he's leading me through some back alley and if I fail to catch up and start falling far behind, I'll lose him at some turn. I shuffle as fast as I can shuffle. I brush away drooping leaves when they block my blurry view of him, and they slap my neck wet when they spring back. When the largest and droopiest and most dramatic of twisting vines come between me and Neyo, I butterfly my arms like I'm parting tall grass in the savanna, and what meets me on the other side of the wet lush is the spray from the waterfall I just tried to defeat. I am high up on a cliff.

"You're brave, ma'am," Neyo shouts through the white noise of the waterfall. "At three, ma'am. At three!"

"No!"

"Ma'am, the only way back to your family is to jump."

For someone who enjoyed the quiet parameters of social distancing and who unplugs appliances when it storms and who didn't travel much (or well) until recently, being here at all already feels supernatural. And now to the left and to the right of me, men, women, teenagers, and tweens morph into sprites and do what's rendered me speechless, and jump. One by one, they step up to the edge, fall in, disappear in a cloud of moisture and air, then reemerge, bobbing downstream with expressions recognizable even from where I am. With the long game in mind, I think of my full evolution: where I am from, what I've survived, what hasn't killed me, what's actually made me stronger, where I hope to be, who I hope to be there with. Nothing on the meandering course says I'm a coward. Being careful, because you've had to be many times over, doesn't necessarily, automatically, mean that you're afraid.

And all that the universe is left with after that is a moving image of me in my pink swim dress, the skirt of it flouncing around me as I leap. My hair shoots up like stamens in a lily, my legs needle down like a thin stem, and I am a flower falling to the water, trusting that when she lands, her softness will be caught by another's. Anouk, who has my phone and her Polaroid, takes a shot from where she stands at the rocks—for posterity, for luck. It's a photo of her mother rewilding, a picture of a nation recovering. It's a capture of light: an impression of self-love.

PART IV

REENTRY
Puerto Princesa, Palawan, Philippines

Land of the Batak and Tagbanua,
the island of my dreams,
where my senses come alive

—January 2023

Dispatches from Recovery

2024

We're onto bargaining: To maintain the freelance job that affords this reality, I need to be fast like the woman who ran this house was fast. To run this house, I need to be able to do nine or so things at once, wear nine or so hats in a single day. To write what she wrote—memoirs and travel essays—I must have an intact, reliable memory, plus an ability to recall words and an agile way with them. I need to be in the middle of life, not here in this padded cell that is my physical and mental comfort, and I need to have experiences worth memoir-ing about. Who would care to read a story in which the most exciting scene is that of a woman remembering her name who must try so hard to remember it every day? They say the word essay *comes from the French for "to try," and that makes me want to believe I'm not so far removed from her work and person as I think myself to be. I hope.*

Dr. Hubbard and Dr. Lena and all the other neurosurgeons, neurologists, and neuropsychologists whose names I forget all agree and declare that with time, I will recover most, if not all, the abilities the woman who bought this house and furnished it and whose face appears on travel photos on the fridge once had. It is when they say such things that my anger is the hottest. Time, *they say. Time! As if time were free. As if anyone really had it. As if the woman whose work is curling up at the edges and is yellowing on the kitchen island hadn't ever been robbed of time. But that I have, and that I can give her, and maybe if we shared it, I wouldn't feel so othered from her.*

14

A Beautiful Morning

What is twenty years to deep time? To continental drifts and to magma rising? To the time it takes for a piece of southern China to break off and float off and merge with the oceanic crust that fought its way up from the depths of the Pacific? What are two decades when it takes millennia for limestone and granite to intrude and protrude through even older igneous rock? To their maturation into mountain? To the welcoming of a new age with the open hand of a cliff, a cliff that will fold and form life lines and heart lines as those in a palm, crevices in which dirt will fit and saplings will take root and dream to become rainforest? What is twenty years to the time it takes for animals to multiply and evolve, for the flora around them to propagate into what we now call "biodiversity" and for it all to wilt and wither back to the earth, to become earth? To the eras spent carrying and feeling the feet of generation upon generation of beasts? To the span of time it took to get used to being shaken by the growl of a to-be-extinct tiger announcing its having crossed here on a land bridge? What are two decades when for so long the rainforest let itself sprawl and receive rain and let water collect in lagoons and let a part of it rive through? Another era: Verb then becomes noun, from *rive* to *river*, a dynamic body sustaining kingdoms and queendoms of Austronesian peoples. What is twenty years to the time it takes for the river to stretch longer, for rainforest to sprawl some more, only to shrink again because the colonizers have come? This is when time quickens, when what they call history marks itself as years, days, hours. This is when it begins: forgetting that we are part of an ancient and collective hum, forgetting that parts and particles of us belong in pockets in other eons.

In Palawan, where I am on this fourth hour of this January day, the sun has not risen, but in the waning moonlight prefacing its coming, I can see four seats as my solid options: a cushioned settee, two wooden chairs around a bamboo tea table, and a porch swing. I've stepped out onto the patio branching off our luxury villa. And I don't know what to do with myself. I've never rented a villa, luxury or otherwise, and especially not one that boasts a private entrance to a semiprivate pool shared only by seven guests on the west side of what a veteran traveler might call a "sleepy" resort. I also have not, since I left my country at age sixteen, lounged in a chair or any similar kind of furniture or fitting in these islands whose trees sway in an unforgivably soothing way. I need to sit. I need to sit because if I don't, my knees will give and when my loves wake up from the post-travel slumber they have found but I have not, they will find me kneeling on and kissing and pounding the ground, shriveled like a raisin in a puddle of my own tears, crying again because I am as furious as I am grateful. But, of course, this is all too dramatic, too much for my recovering body. I am not actually a woman who kneels on the ground and kisses it and pounds it. I am, instead, the frequent but quiet crier whose steno pad is flecked with tearstains at the NGO all-hands while she presents, still effectively and impressively, a video dispatch from cat-5 Hurricane Dorian. I am the writer who works on a memoir at the neighborhood bakery, the baker and his cashier going about their over-the-counter bagel orders, neither sympathetic or unsympathetic to the regular who comes every weekday and sniffles as she types away. I am the parent so touched by all the children's poems, her collar is wet even before her own daughter steps up to the microphone to read a poem she's kept a surprise, a poem containing lines like *my parents / like lightbulbs / illuminate me.* I am an open crier. A leaky tap. A soft person easily brought to tears and not the mouthy, ranting, rightfully detonative matriarch persona my birth mother and birth sister have siphoned from a favorite prime-time teleserye. I am not a version of the memeable Filipina American immigrant mom, yelling as she walks in from rather exploitative work, welcomed home by unfolded laundry and uncooked rice and threatening to throw a slipper at some ingrato's face. I've been spared from, or perhaps loved and written and therapied out of, this very near and looming possibility.

In my orbit, I've long normalized crying. And on this awaited two-week vacation, what will become most unremarkable, at least to me and to my two, are the wet eyelashes and the puffy lids and the red nose. I will wear them like my wedding ring, unnoticeable until absent, a signature accessory containing story and meaning. When servers or boat skippers or retail clerks glance a second too long, tempted to wonder why, all I'll say is "Twenty years na po mula nung umalis ako." And they'll *hmm*, and nothing more, because the thought of having been away that long is both inconceivable and believable, for many reasons that to them I need not name, and they'll hand me the coffee or the life vest or my change, and we'll all go on about our days because I am just another Filipina making her way back, slipping into the comforts of home.

When I decide to sit on the porch swing, it begins again. Tears fall. They plop out of my eyes and dribble to my jaw, hanging there for a second before they drip for my clavicles to catch. The kindness I offer myself is exactly what's been taken from me: time. I will sit in this swing for almost two hours, allowing myself the silent but not inexpressive act of catharsis. When the median between you and a culture is an abusive parent, it's easier to sever yourself from the toxicity that you might confuse as the heart of a collective identity than it is to sit in the momentary discomfort of meeting a place again for the first time.

When I mind for how long I've been crying, when I begin to think it might be selfish and self-indulgent and that I must stop, I clear my throat because I quickly remember that sitting here with my tears is a kind of kindness, that Brown softness is a kind of justice.

From behind me, the wind nudges. We go on this way, me kicking back and the wind pushing forward, a couple of hours of solitary child's play, a simple game. Forth and back, forth and back, lulling just like that, my toes grazing cold tile and my hair catching both the January breeze and the day's first rays. The sun is fully awake now, so is the town, and I begin to hear a pool boy whistle while he works. I smell garlic frying. My baby hairs stand up when I feel a small panic because I haven't yet put on my uniform and I haven't yet brushed my teeth and I might be late for school, and I'll surely get yelled at by my mama or her lover. Then I remember: I am thirty-six (and a half) now, a mother.

The sliding doors crack open. A little tan foot pokes through. The next I see are my most favorite pair of crusty morning eyes, the most comforting of tangled morning hair. My tears are still coming, softly still, and Anouk is unafraid of them. She walks toward me and the swing, and being here together has become, in no time at all, the most everyday thing.

Before she sits with me, she skims the light-blue pool water, light as this morning's honesty, and scoops out a floating kalachuchi flower. When she joins me in my play place and cuddles in close, twirling the white bloom in her fingers, I get a little spritz from it and smell the honeysuckle fragrance that is as reminiscent of yesteryear as the grueling, triggering days are. Like the earth, like this land, like my country and its wonders, there is so much of me that can be restored, that's already received healing goodness.

The days didn't all go to the dogs. I try, because I still can. The twenty years didn't all deplete me. We are not completely severed from the ancient collective hum. The song is longer still, and Spirit deeper. It is not too late to sit in a swing or to have the sensitive urge to be one with the morning. It is not beyond reality to be returned, not at all beyond it for daybreak to have no purpose outside of a good, long cry, for the eons and the eras to collapse into the single, dainty mass of a flower, and for it to be twirled in a soulmate's fingers and to rest in the folds of her palm, to have nothing to occupy you outside your wanting and your craving for knock-you-off-your-feet Barako coffee.

The pool boy's whistle sounds louder, closer, and it's because he and his net have made it to our end of the pool. He looks up from his devotion, notices that we are there. I'm certain he can tell that I've been crying, but all he says is, because today should be like any day, and he somehow knows it, "Magandang umaga po," which means, in our language, a beautiful morning.

Dispatches from Recovery

2024

Take it easy, *people say in their messages and cards, as if none of us were conditioned to believe that rest is earned, not deserved. When I sit down to read the manuscript, all I can think of is how tired she must've been, the woman whose feet fit the shoes collecting dust by the door. But also, when I read her stories, I'm strengthened by her willingness to experiment with leisure, to toy with the concept of travel. Because she went places, despite the precarity it invited and all its material and figurative costs, I can believe that I, too, can venture out of the limits of my comfort, even if all that means is embracing this time to convalesce. Because she went home, I can inch closer to the belief that I, too, can return to a way of being that feels less foreign.*

15

Breakfast Buffet Included

Palawan swings out to the west of its sister provinces and islands, like a sash untying itself from a long sequined dress, inviting us to consider that while the sparkles dotting toward the equator are worth the hype, it's the emphatic poise and narcotic elegance of a slender and latitudinal peninsula that deserve our eyes and mind. I've chosen to come here instead of spending our holiday in my birth city of Manila for reasons most simply and effectively explained in this way: The metro is small, and the past lives there. To travel across the world to it is to parachute into a fire with a backpack of baseless beliefs that your learnings and age can snuff out the blaze that nearly consumed you as a child. (Read: Puerto Rico.) Of course, this blaze is less the historic, zesty, buzzling city and more my aging, sizzling, bullshitting mother, who may or may no longer live there but whose location is less the matter than her influence that tentacles through. Since my departure from the Philippines, she has committed more crimes and embezzled more family and family-friend money than she did when I was under her care, and I know this through the carrier pigeon that is her only other living child, my now Britain-based older brother who no longer has to steal candy for me.

In college, while I was undocumented and surviving by working off the books as a café hostess, a speakeasy server, a babysitter, and a tutor, all at once, my estranged mother received news about me through the free roaming and wireless service that is the Ilocano-Filipino-American gossip network. She learned of my continued resourcefulness and lucrative skills. Not only did she receive bits of my life to puff her up, but she also got intel she could wager. She decided to tell me by email that she had breast cancer, *the* cancer that dominated and continues to dominate our family tree. Of course, it was believable. Of course, it was false. But when I hadn't yet known that the "diagnosis" was yet another one of her scams, I wired her money through Western Union on every payday, about $200 (or two of 1-0-0) each time, which then was the amount I would've spent on a month's groceries.

The longhand: My mother was not sick, never sick, not in the genuine care-for-your-elders way, and at my heaviest then, I was 102 pounds at five foot three. I ate one good and free meal a day at the café where I was working, and at night I ate one fried egg for dinner and a lick of Nutella for dessert. I was so small, people mistook me for a middle schooler. At the café, when I asked guests if they had made reservations, it took them a moment to realize that I was an adult and not the owner's child helping out on a weekend. When my brother found me on Facebook just months after graduation, I had shrunk to my smallest and been financially abused by our mama for several semesters and through ascents from babysitter to nanny and from hostess to brunch manager, plus a new but still off-the-books job as an art critic's researcher. I was not only risking my safety and ability to stay in America by being at these jobs but also making myself yet again prey to the woman who birthed me and thought of me as a resource the way the United States saw my country as something to persuade into "consensual" exploration, extraction, and exploitation. Predators, they're all the same, I tell ya. My mother was always ready to start a fire, and she used me repeatedly like the back of a matchbook, striking against my bareness to feed her pyromania.

Ever original, ever a champion of language and style, she deserved nothing less than the fitting repayment of my giving new meaning to the phrase "burning bridges." When my brother woke me up from the spell of her non-cancer, the information wormed in my brain until it got to a mostly formed prefrontal cortex. I was twenty-four and had just married and had just conceived a child. I was still undocumented, because, my god, those papers take a while and they required money, which, if I haven't made clear, my mother pilfered from me.

But by then I knew to cut the proverbial cord and to hope to plant my end of it somewhere safer and more deserving of my worst and best. I thought, as early as then and while still unbeknownst to me that I would come home to the Philippines at some point, that I could redefine the "mother" and "land" in "motherland" the way my mother used to play with words and toy with semantics. Like all things toxic from my past and from our postcolonial culture, I would bypass the greedy middleman and go straight to the source. Palawan maintains 50 percent of its original forest cover and continues to be home to the "last true" or uncolonized Filipinos, the Tagbanua. If we're talking preservation of nature and culture, Palawan is it. If we're talking preservation of self, the answer, at least for me, lands there too. It's truly a no-brainer. So yes, okay, I heard Manila has changed much, and "for the better" and that my mother might live north of there now, maybe, but who wants to spend a hard-earned—and I mean *hard-earned*—holiday brushing against the mental triggers that a place could hold. I had and have to venture beyond.

So Palawan it was, the island of my dreams. Puerto Princesa, its capital, was a lovely compromise in that you could, if you wanted, call it a city, but you could, as most do, ascribe it as paradise. *Where you, all of you, come alive.* It's my first breakfast here, and I shall savor, because when you've starved yourself for years so you could pay for your mother's nonexistent chemo and radiation bills and you wear proudly every pound you've since gained and are several email address changes from her contact, you find a table for three in the open-air dining room, under the trellised awning and facing the largest of the pools. You pick a seat that allows you to stare down, on one side, said pool, and on the other, a U-shaped buffet that starts with an ube waffle station and ends with tiered serving platters of mango and coconut sticky rice. You pan the camera through your eyes and you take in all the purples, yellows, and greens. Ready, set, and just before the go: You swallow whole the air blowing in from the nearby rainforest.

As soon as we give our drink order—two coffees and a hot chocolate—Stephen, Anouk, and I get up from the wicker seats and walk to the midpoint of the buffet, inadvertently cutting the U-shaped breakfast line that crests at the steaming chafing dishes of fluffy, crunchy golden-brown garlic rice. Apologies are in order, but the lady behind us smiles and flicks her hand at us, instructing us to, "Sige, sige, go ahead." Her other hand holds a used plate, proof of a second helping. We're hungrier, more eager, more deprived.

I mouth, *Salamat po.*

I bless my two with scoopfuls, the metal serving spoon filmy from garlic acid, frying oil, and rice steam. It's a kind of scepter with particular powers. As thanks, they bow slightly. When the smell of fried garlic rises to fog up Stephen's glasses, he jokes, "Mmm-mm, blindingly good," and it's just the cheeky, corny humor we need at the outset. I direct him to the next row of dishes, to where the viands of cured meats and fried or dried fishes are, and when I do so by using my pursed lips as pointers, I'm just one of many Pinay mothers here giving instructions in this way. It's something I never lost, a card always in the back pocket, waiting to be pulled out. Lips for pointers: a telltale sign of a lola, a tita, an ate, or a Filipina/x mom. And, as well, something my old classmate would have also shamed me for. If she saw me now, she might say, rolling her eyes and flipping her hair, *So low-class,* which, in *that* language, means "too close to our uncolonized truth."

My first plate is a mound of garlic rice topped with the oniony, glassy vermicelli of pancit bihon, plus a side of fried banana. It's how I've always known and wanted to structure my meals: a big savory-and-sweet breakfast; a lunch of rice and proteins swimming in deep, dark, unctuous gravy; a merienda of cheesy or fruity bread; and a supper so light, it's really just an aperitif to the next morning's meal. When I'd graduated from affording meals by way of Coke bottle deposits and started living with my half sister, or my father's first child from his first marriage, I adopted our people's routine. A big breakfast, a hearty lunch, a happy snack, a dinner just to cleanse the palate. It's one of my sister's gifts I will always be thankful for. But this order is not the preferred prix fixe, so to speak, in America, and the workaday lifestyle there rarely allows for a leisurely breakfast, and so while the La Quintas and Holiday Inns of day trips past will never measure up to the design and amenities of this four-star Palawan resort, the all-you-can-eat breakfast buffets they offered served as little beads on a rosary string, little devotions, little stones to step on one after the other, until I could make my way here, to the meal that echoes, thus far, everyone's and everything's *Welcome home.*

Stephen and Anouk got the memo, it seems. They each have a large plate, two dessert plates, and a bowl, each one filled to the brim with gingery broth or piled high with sugary brioches called ensaymada. We don't talk. We do look up between bites just to flash a smile, but outside these quick exchanges, there's pretty much nothing else worth doing at the moment other than eat. He eats. She eats. I eat. We'll eat like this for the next ten mornings, and when I watch them engorge on the food that makes me feel like I've come back to a self that has yearned to reacquaint with me, it's the most appropriate and most healing and most holistic use of an old Philippine saying: Nakakataba ng puso. Fattening the heart.

Second servings, third servings, and, because Neyo was right in saying I'm brave, a fourth for good measure. What's so brave is not what might outwardly look like conquest, like I'm attacking the buffet. The valiance lies in the wanting to feed myself, over and over and over again, unbothered by the calories, uninhibited by cost (*Included in the package! Good exchange rates!*), and, most of all, unrelenting to the controlling forces and abusive maneuverings of someone who should have wanted good for me, who should have wished me full, who should have been my protector, provider, and good dinner company. What the past didn't allow, the present is making a big show of. Time is not only full of tricks; it's also quite an attention whore. Bells, whistles, benign pyrotechnics. Every slurp, every bite, is a music festival in my mouth. They're altogether returning to me every remitted 2-0-0, plus more.

To not expect reproof. To do unquantifiable things.

Just when I think I'm done, finally done, finally, finally, fi-na-lly, the back-of-house rolls out through the kitchen's double metal doors a vat on a dolly, and Anouk points because, how could it be? There are vats on dollies everywhere here where her mom is from. "Ma! Mom! Look!"

Boiled peanuts are not usually a morning staple here, so when the curious cauldron has been rolled to its designated spot, I push my chair out so fast, I make the floor screech. Anouk follows. She and I investigate and, on tiptoe, peer in. And, again, time likes to make a show. It likes to make an advertisement of itself. I cup my hand over my mouth. It's like I've just looked into a mystical well. Silent tears yet again fall. A server hands me a bowl and offers to scoop the surprise for me. I nod. He nods, as though he understands that I've spent a good portion of the last decade culturally isolated in the very white coastal "top city" that is Charleston, South Carolina. He plunges down the ladle. When it emerges from the depths of the vat, from where it seems my emotions have fallen and melted, it's steaming and overflowing with sweet goo and sticky rice. On early mornings at my elementary school, before the school officially opened and when my mother had to leave me somewhere so she could have a longer day for her escapades and crimes, one of the canteen cooks would share the staff breakfast with me. The kindness of others, along with my smarts, I guess, was how I survived then. On those mornings, if it wasn't fried kamote, it was this: champorado, or what some might translate as chocolate rice porridge.

I bring my bowl to our table and pour milk from a little ceramic beaker. Instinctively, like it's yesterday, I swirl in the creaminess with a dessert spoon and make my own Milky Way in a humble bowl. Puffs of rice, ribbons of milk, the depths of dark chocolate. Before me are the cosmos in miniature, and my mother is lost somewhere in it, I don't know where. I give it another swirl, to obscure her whereabouts further. My two watch as I spoon out a bite and bring the universes to my mouth. It's a chocolate bomb of bittersweet. It's smooth until it sticks. It's definitely not soup. Made from scratch, it's not quite custard nor a pudding but the friendly in-between. The way they've made it here at Princesa Garden gives it a coconutty endnote to coat my tongue while my teeth smack and tack at each other. It's everything I had waited twenty years for it to be. And it's mine.

Dispatches from Recovery

2024

"But you do have time," the grief therapist says, in my opinion, dismissively. I hear shuffling in the background and suspect she's doing a chore while on this call. I wonder to myself, Is that the sound of a coffee grinder or a washing machine? *I get distracted, as I'm prone to do now with my "borderline" attention, and begin to think about the laundry piled on the bed. And then she says, like I'm the one who's done something to offend, "You're here now, are you not?"*

16

Healing Waters

Rare species that we are. Rested ones, I mean. And the surest and clearest of signs of such is how we three are choosing to spend this late morning together but separate. A mutual solitude.

Stephen is kayaking just on the other side of the bamboo bridge connecting our villa to the white sand beach, probably talking to himself while eyeing blue starfish. Or, equally probable, he's talking *to* the blue starfish. The idle, restless, hiding trauma response, lethargic version of him that surfaced in Puerto Rico is long gone, and he's alive to himself and his surroundings, so much so that he is, I bet, already planning his next adventure. He's gotten so good at making plans.

He planned this whole trip: from our eHealthPasses and thirty-six-hour PCR tests to the villa and the package that includes four excursions and the breakfast buffet. It's so nice to see a loved one who wears his jeans and boxers until they're embarrassingly threadbare buy up, choose the option costing thirty-six dollars more, and book the place that comes with a rain showerhead and daily upkeep of fresh flowers. The message his upbringing pummeled into him and that he's unlearning is that he's undeserving of preferences: knowing them, voicing them, choosing them.

Also nice is my current view of Anouk. She swims a stone's throw from me, scooping imaginary jellies and, as well, talking to herself. She's in some kind of synchronized swim choreography with a floating leaf and the shadows cast from its mother tree, and whatever she's saying is certainly being heard because, my god, they are, truly, moving in and on water on some beat I can't hear but can see.

And as for me, well, as I'll have it any day if I could, I'm knee-deep in pool water, my lower limbs dangling off the edge of our villa patio and my hands catching the embossed back and front covers of a memoir about a half-Filipina mother traveling to Europe. I swing my legs as I read. I'm very happy for this fellow mother and fellow writer, and I'm happy for me, and the ode I give to us both is to read her pages aloud but softly, filling the air with my soft-spokenness and with stories about these ventures, speaking them and speaking them until they become the air. Until stories of immigrant women traveling for pleasure and self-discovery are as normal as oxygen, there for us all to breathe.

Capitalism would urge me to compete with her, to have thoughts about her book's existence as a threat to the one I'm writing, but I'm stronger because I am softer, and comparison, thank the gods, is not my language, not anymore. Twenty years in America and I know that a free market, and the "healthy" competition it fosters, rarely equates to a people who are free. I am thinking now of Frederick Douglass and any and all who've pondered the paradox of "the land of opportunity." "What to the slave is the Fourth of July?" Douglass asked. "We pray for America, land of the tired," we used to pray at Catholic school-wide Holy Rosary. The richest country in the world, or "the experiment" as some might call it, was built on stolen land, enslavement, and waves of imported or outsourced cheap labor, one group encouraged to despise and defeat the others. Competition has always been part of the white supremacist and patriarchal design. Indigenous peoples, Blacks, and other people of color or people born elsewhere have long withstood all this, as well as resisted this age-old exploitation through rebellions and protests of many kinds: some through sit-ins and walkouts, others through litigation and legislation, some more necessarily violent than others and at other times manifesting as resting and living beautiful, glorious lives.

And here now, back on this side of the ocean, my hair gathered gracefully on one side and my solitude so intact, I am unwearied and unhurried. And this too, I remember, is protest.

Our physical break from the United States, as short as the past thirty or so hours have been, doubles as a mental break from its mechanisms and machinations, and I can already feel, in the small of my back, a release so deep. The numbing vibrations usually traveling up and down my spine and shooting across my right hip and down my leg have left my body, and I'm already hearing better in my left ear, my bad ear, and I am certain that my hearing trouble is connected to my back pain is connected to my throat disease is connected to my immigrant heartache.

Anouk's hips, I also don't doubt, are getting the aqua-massage they deserve after a whole day scrunched in a plane seat. *Healing waters* was how I described it to Anouk not long ago. And I'd remind her now, but she's currently curling and uncurling like a shrimp in shallow water, whirlpooling it that the leaf circles her, and there's no point reminding her at all because, it seems, she knows and she knows and she knows.

She's doing what a child should be doing: being oblivious to her parents', or anyone's, stress. Another rarity: an immigrant's child not sharing an adult's burden.

And Stephen and I, we just keep surprising ourselves. It turns out we know how to be oblivious to stress too, even if it's just today and the day after and the day after then. It took a while to get here, to knowing that resting was a part of our freedom, to making a few definitive choices including professional U-turns and personal boundaries, but anyhow, here we are, we are here, we made it.

"Mama, come in the water!"

She only has to ask once. I use my hotel key card as a bookmark and set my book down. I swish my way in. Three times, I say aloud but softly, my moving lips just a quiver above the water, "She knows and she knows and she knows."

Healing waters. Incantatory.

Dispatches from Recovery

2024

"You have time to heal," Stephen assures me. He, Buki, and Nancy put together an online fundraiser to cover whatever losses in income the brain injury has caused. Family, friends, friends of friends, acquaintances, readers, editors, writing students, my hairstylist, total strangers—they all went to the web page and came to the rescue, dollar for dollar, matching the amount struck through in a cell in a spreadsheet in the computer Stephen was instructed to gather from the emergency room that horrid day, the day the world spun.

17

Honey Hunting

I am looking for God wherever I can. Even now, while I, as one does on vacation, order a midday coffee.

In my youth, I was an acolyte, or my mother at least wanted me to be. On Wednesdays, therefore, she woke me up at four o'clock by pulling my blanket off me, and I would suddenly feel cold and exposed. Clammy in the school uniform I'd slept in, a trick I played to appease her, to make her think I was as eager to go to midweek sunrise Mass, I already smelled of sweat before the day even started. But Mama demanded efficiency those mornings, and if you didn't want to be the subject of her Catholic confession and the object of her subsequent penance, you acted with and from the understanding that not cleanliness but promptness was next to godliness. She wanted one thing on those mornings: first pew, middle seat. You made haste. If you were smart and wanted to survive another day, you helped to get her to that pew and that seat, even if it meant looking like a crumpled and sticky cough drop wrapper at the posh school she couldn't afford with her dirty money and so she has you afford it through your cunning and awards.

The next thing she wanted, after the front-row seat to not that Madonna but *that* Madonna, was for me to fall in line with the other overachieving prepubescents and reach out my hand to receive my morning's responsibility. The golden chalice and bejeweled cross were, of course, the primest and shiniest of commodities, but to have been handed the donation basket was enough to keep my mother's heart palpitations from being conjured and shaking up the room. Besides, I liked to count the cash. I aimed my hand at that basket. I liked to see who gave what, how much, whose peso bill was as dilapidated and tarnished as my school uniform. How much a Filipino would give to the Christian cause. We were starving, and I wondered if nobody else was.

Even then, I was an observer, an investigator, a collector of information. I was writing stories about the churchgoers in my head. I think my mother had a little pride for me those Wednesdays, mistaken that my little mouth movements were from the little softly uttered prayers I'd hoarded in my heart the first half of the week. She had a sense that I had an otherworldly sense, that I felt spirits or saw the ghost of her dead child or dead father or could communicate with the angels. She felt closer to God with me as a tagalong, a talisman. Like her looks, her Catholicism was more Roman than Philippine, and my darker skin and small nose maybe made her believe I was more "native" and interacted with the supernatural in ways she couldn't, and she wanted it all, all the luck and favor she could have, Roman or Indigenous or whatnot. And I could do all that, the seeing and the sensing and the communicating, but what kept me from dipping back into my sleep those Wednesday mornings were not chants or petitions but the stories I made up about the woman with the mole on her lip, the couple with matching canes, and the priest himself, with whom all the rest of them were besotted because he was the history of that shrine embodied, the junction of the Church and the Revolution, a professed member of the Dominican Order, and an organizer, a protestor against autocracy in 1986 and 2001, when dictatorships and sweeping ratifications to the law threatened our basic freedoms. My storytelling, my language, my faith, my fight for freedom. Do you see it now? They'd always been tied to survival, and they'd always been fused to each other.

Midweek Mass was shorter and a lot less showy than Sunday's, and with a smaller head count of devotees, the priest could host it at the smaller of the chapels at the Shrine for Mary, Queen of Peace. It was a dark room with only the orange flicker of a few candles and the glowing red of the incense bowl to give shape to the bodies and wooden furniture sweating and swelling in the dim. It was so cavernous, when people prayed out loud and read off their novena cards, it sounded like bellows, like howls.

The thing was, my mother was actually bellowing, actually howling. But she camouflaged. They thought her passionate, devout. I found her terrifying, especially then. There's no fear like the fear you feel when witnessing your mother display the sadness that forged her mischief and malfeasance. There's no greater responsibility than knowing something about your mother that nobody else could know. Aside from Wednesday church, her other devotion involved the extremes.

My brother and I feared her because she had no middle ground. *On brand,* as they say. We were either bathing in cash or broke. She was either dressed too hot in layers too thick for a smoggy city like Manila or pruning her orchids nippy in a sheer camisole. My mother was an accumulation of frustrations with all things pedestrian, not excluding the roles of nurturer, provider, adviser, and friend. She hated having to be these medians, which, of course, were the very roles I would later fill and be my most comfortable in.

Those Wednesdays, her prayers at times turned into wailing and arm throwing with her body doubling over so far toward the floor, her hair touching the cushioned rests meant for kneeling. When she moaned and folded her body like that, like she was in an exorcism, the woman with the mole, the couple with the canes, and the priest with the fighter spirit would all look to me for an explanation. I gave them none. I looked busy, like I couldn't be distracted from the counting of bills. Even then, I knew that saying nothing or saying just enough could save, if not your life, your family's reputation, which, postcolonial nation that we are, was as synonymous as an American identity and what an American does for a living.

As the sun rose, the bells rang. Midweek Mass ended. The priest told us, in the name of the Father and of the Son and of the Holy Spirit, to go in peace to love and serve the Lord, which I, a child still, took as an admonition to keep myself safe from Mama, my mama safe from the world, and the world safe from her.

At Mass's end, my mother unfolded herself, slowly, like a tulip in a vase following light through a window at dawn, and she gathered herself as she gathered her hair in a high bun, and she sniffed until her snot was hidden far up in the black of her nostrils, where whatever else could not be seen in the light of day must be concealed. A veteran criminal, she knew how not to leave a trace. I trailed behind her as she exited the shrine and as she hailed a cab and headed out to whatever con job she had laid out for herself that day. I crossed the street to school and entered another set of gates and threw myself into the beginnings of my robotic productivity, armed with a backpack of my brother's old pencils and a subconscious formed by mornings with her in that shrine, which was a monument for the Filipino quest for freedom from exploitation, a freedom anchored in spirituality. I worked hard all day, gave my all at soccer and at schoolyard games to distract myself from the unpalatable truth that no matter how cruel and disconcerting she was, I wanted her. I should say now, I am always looking for God, and my mother, wherever I can.

These two beings I've distanced myself from are also, consistently, the two I'm most expectant for even when they've continually failed me. Less and less do I see their hands in my life, but more and more I understand that both would always ache for me, and I feel this ache throbbing always. I wait for it. It's the last slurp through my reusable straw at the sad end of my morning iced coffee, the thrum of a subway approaching a lonely platform in off-peak hours, and the way my house in Charleston croaks twice and just twice at exactly four o'clock every morning. Secure in a marital and familial love I've formed with Stephen and Anouk, I am no longer afraid of this longing for me, no longer think it could, like a thief in the night, snatch me from the world I've made, and I allow it in the same spaces I'm trying to now color with the wild paintbrush of my adamant delight. Alert but not enslaved to it, it's not a haunting. Like Stephen's father's anger and his mother's low-frequency fear, it is just an occasional, not defining, feature of my life. I can go on, and I do. I work, I earn, and I pay for things, some more frivolous than others, some Instagrammable for the mere heck of it, like this coffee concoction made with Palawan honey approaching our table.

Sourced deep from within the Palawan rainforest, the Philippines' last ecological frontier, nectar from the gods of the Tagbanua flavors my drink. Honing the skill from the age of ten, Tagbanua honey hunters say an ancient prayer kept this secret from outsiders before each harvest. Then they set off into the bush, in search of rare stingless bees feeding on endemic tropical flowers I've never before heard of nor seen. The coffee itself comes served as ice cubes in a chilled tumbler, meant to melt once the warm milk and honey ribbon down the glass.

I haven't waited twenty years to taste it again, as I did with the champorado. This time, it's a first. It's something that in my childhood I didn't have the chance of sampling. When I sip the first sip, which is a long sip because why withhold, I do taste the gifts of this ecoregion, plus more. It's hard to tell apart the Barako, coffee introduced by the Spanish in 1740, floral and citrusy and just acidic but dark, from the honey, sap produced from precolonial human and prehistoric insect traditions. This drink is like the yearning of my mother and of the god of my youth, which are there, always, mingled now with my waking and making, the weft and warp of my past and forthcoming joy. I look for them where I can, as I look now for pleasure.

I clink Anouk's ube ice-cream bowl with my teaspoon and gesture an invitation to a toast. She licks the back of her spoon before setting it down on a saucer. She raises her bowl. A fear of good things sprouts behind my ears, then disappears, as I knew it would. I raise my glass. I raise it to all the things that I have mostly but not fully lost, to the ties that bind and to all that they marry. To everything I am still searching for.

Dispatches from Recovery

2024

"Do you have time?" asks the girl who is just home from school and smells like a classroom. "Can you help me with my homework?"

"Of course," I tell her—and myself—"I have time."

Her homework is for English class and the assignment is to write a flash-fiction piece in which the protagonist is confronted with a time constraint.

"You gotta be kidding me," I say under my breath.

"Why are you smiling? What's so funny?" she asks.

"Not a thing," I tell her, and proceed to explain the basics of a story: A character has a desire and challenging that desire or the pursuit of it are many factors, such as other characters, other conflicting interests, physical barriers like a broken bridge or flat tire or rain or a brain aneurysm rupture. Also posing challenges to a character's wants or needs are abstract things like fear or shame and, yes, time, or in the case of the assignment at hand, the limited amount of such.

"Hmm," she says, "my character desires . . . concert tickets!"

"And let me guess," I say, "she only has the tiniest window of time to buy them?"

From here she riffs: "Oh and of course the day to buy them is the day she is late for the bus home! And her cat, that silly cat, jumps on her laptop keyboard as she's about to hit the Buy button!"

And I riff: "And the laptop isn't charged; it's dying!"

"And she can't find her charger!"

"Never mind the charger—the whole house is without power!"

"Tick, tick, she has a minute left . . ."

"Her phone still has a charge and—"

And we finish the story right at the teacher's expected word count.

"Ma," she says, "look! We did it! We're such a good team! And you, Ma, it's like you've been doing this your whole life!"

18

Fireflies in the Night

We're on a small bangka with half our tour group, about ten of us, moving farther away from the main boat with its motor, lamps, and general feeling of security. Slowly we head into the pitch-black, leaving behind the lights of Puerto Princesa, the bargaining and haggling sounds of its night market, and the corral of handsy, smoochy teens publicly displaying their awkwardness and affection. As we forge deeper down a strait dividing a forested islet, a silence falls upon us: a kind of collective respect for the dark that could consume us should we fail to do what the tour guide had practiced with us on land. Speak and make sounds only when told, keep all body parts inside the dinghy, dim phone screens, and shut off camera flashes. Save for a retired Serbian solo traveler, the tour group is made up of balikbayans, and we understand that nature here is god and goddess, and we enter at our own risk. "Tabi tabi po," I say under my breath as the air changes: fresher but thicker, smelling less of salt and more of moss.

I can't even look to see how Anouk is doing, if she's scared, because it's that dark. When I hold up my hand before me, just inches from my face, I can't see it, and I can't see that I've held it up so close to the back of her head. I accidentally smack her as I bring my hand back down, and she doesn't react, but I do, and there I am again, the delinquent at Charleston crabbing and the food-poisoned in Fort Lauderdale and the nearly drowned in Jamaica waterfall chasing, and I am, without meaning to, the apologetic tourist who is better off shutting up than repeating, "Sorry, sorry, sorry." And I can't see them, but I can feel that my two are trying not to laugh, are shaking their heads. Thank goodness no one can see my face, and maybe when we reemerge out of the mangroves and into the light, they'll mistake somebody else for me, and I can still be friendly on vacation, and I'll get to tell them the grand purpose of this journey. But for now, I'll be the opposite of grand. I hush myself. I don't move even when my nose itches.

When the little riot I've created dies down, the boat nudges on again. Our forward movement is at the mercy of a boat skipper manning a twenty-foot bamboo pole half submerged in brackish water. We move in heaves. I have a little private panic when I think of what we'll do should he lose grip of the pole, if it disappears into the water. I swat away mental images of Jennifer Lopez wrestling an anaconda. I try to recall, for feelings of self-efficacy, that I've swum against white-water currents and jumped off a mossy cliff and made a twenty-year return to my birthplace, and there's really no fear I can't face. I'll swim myself and my child back to the larger boat should I need to. Travel makes you braver because it halts, or at least dilutes, your fear not of what's out there but of what you thought you didn't already have within you. The greatest of lengths always point back inside.

When the ocean sounds are out of our hearing, cricket sounds seize the night. I suddenly feel fortified. I am ready. I paid close attention to our prior training, and when the tour guide says to, I'll call to the fireflies just as he said we should, and I'll invite their response. His instructions to us were, I admit, rather quirky, but I'm game. My sportiveness and cheeriness were exactly what Anouk's needed of late.

During the pandemic, Anouk had written a poem for English class:

> Eyes are drooping / mouth is turned down /
> looking out the winddow / and
> having new friends / new bird friends / blue birds
> / cardinals / and a hawk /
> Singing to me / a bed time story / wihle I miss
> my friends

I tried not to cry during a subsequent Zoom meeting with Anouk's teacher, but it was impossible not to when the piece at the center of the conversation was a wondrously sad work of art: grief in Anouk's language. I learned from her teacher that the "onlys" in her class were twice isolated: separated from their peers and suddenly finding themselves only ever in the company of adults who were crumbling under the weight of an accumulation of new modes of work, parenting, marriage. In other words, she was lost in the company of grown-ups who were just as lost, and at home, wherever she turned, all she saw was disorientation. We ended the call with a chorus of "We're all in this together."

Even now, three years later, I am still haunted by the depth of Anouk's grief, and this trip is an extension of my promise to her and to her teacher to be de facto playful company. When the tour guide asks if we're ready, I sit up straight.

He calls: "China."

We whisper *hello* in Mandarin. We wait.

Little flickers twinkle at us, and we marvel, although discreetly. We applause, silently, puffy palms making puffy sounds, and we grow wide-eyed, the whites of our eyes breaking through the black.

The tour guide then says, "Spain."

We whisper, "Hola."

The forest hedging on both sides glows like the Biltmore covered in LED Christmas lights, stretching long and high and pulsing and blinking as though activated by our voices. Anouk reaches back in search of my hand. She doesn't find it but locates my knee, and when she does, she gives it a squeeze and I know what she's trying to say, "Ma! Mom! Look!"

The tour guide proceeds in coaching us: Germany, Poland, France, Japan, Korea. We respond, like little animatronics programmed in different languages.

Hallo!

Witam!

Bonjour!

Kon'nichiwa!

Annyeonghaseyo!

Glowing, more glowing. The fireflies are everywhere, scintillating. It's a bioluminescent spectacle. I can't believe they really can say hello back. We speak and nature responds, and I feel more connected to it than I have in a long time. The tour guide says the fireflies also respond to song, even though they encamp wherever humans are not. And I think, *Oh, it's because Mother Earth sings to them too, and all songs are a version of the ancient hum, and they must, therefore, enjoy all forms of musicality.* Again, I feel fortified, and so I choose none other than the great Adele, and, still in a whisper, begin to serenade my new insect friends with lines like *Go ea-eahee-eaheehee-ea-sy on me, baby.* The fireflies are delighted, even as my voice cracks, and they reward my performance with a holiday light show.

Before we know it, it's been twenty minutes of lurching forward into the depths of this islet, and we've come to its cul-de-sac. The way out of the mangroves is the way we came in, and again we are at the mercy of a boat skipper and his bamboo. I know of the strength of the fast-growing grass, and still I want to deny its ability to deflect a boatful's weight against the pluff of mud underneath. What if it breaks?

The U-turn is not so effortless. To assuage us and our thoughts, the boat skipper tries to soften his grunts. Every move forward is two creaky, choppy steps back. Jennifer Lopez and her anaconda slither back into the screen of my mind. To help the boat skipper, I lean this way and that, thinking of myself as a ballast or anti-ballast helping to steer us around the murky bend. He hits a solid bed of rocks with the pole, and at long last his push results in a confident advancing. We begin to turn. Slow, climactic, like the approach to the top of a roller coaster when you're holding in place a floating stomach. A collective sigh lifts the boat up off the water when we've finally overcome the roundabout. Feeling the crowd's relief, the tour guide asks if we're ready to again be wowed by nature's pageantry, and our nods are fast and emphatic, disturbing the wet air.

He laughs. Loud, disregarding his own rules. And I suspect everyone else is looking around, searching for context and clues for what to do now.

"My friends," he says, "I have to tell you a secret."

I will flip this boat over, I think to myself, if the lights are actual lights and not fireflies. I allow myself to think that Stephen, this white man I live with and spend my days with and who has planned every one of our days, has just been conned by some tourist trap listed on the internet.

"My friends," the tour guide says again, "the fireflies love your voices, your lovely, lovely singing voices . . ."

Oh dear, I think.

"But they are not responding to your Japanese or your French or your Spanish, ma'am, sir, but to this." A red light flashes by where his voice is coming from, and this whole ride, it turns out, he's been flashing a little red laser, not much bigger than the red laser I bought for our cat, from a hand cupped around his mouth. It's been, and this should be obvious, light responding to light.

The boatful is in an uproar, a happy one; permutations of the same slapstick reaction to the same slapstick joke. We've just been fooled to act like little kindergartners at a puppet show, and we all absolutely fell for it. The Serbian solo traveler mumbles to himself in spurts of Serbian, perhaps admitting how gullible he is. The Filipino Australian mom of two teenagers tries to catch her breath between her chuckles. The teens say, "Mum! Mum," embarrassed by her laugh. I can feel Stephen snicker to himself behind me, his knee jerking against my back. Anouk's breath comes close to my face in the dark, warming where my nose was itching, and she asks if I knew all along. I tell her I had no clue, and she's delighted to know that along with the rest of them, and with her, I'd fallen for the tour guide's cheeky, corny, most effective sense of humor. In the dark, our laughs echo out, our little dinghy rocking with the broken rhythm of our amusement. In the middle of an islet in the middle of the Sulu Sea, under a sky as inky as the water beneath, ten tourists, a tour guide, and a boat skipper disturb the sleep of swimming and slithering and singing creatures.

We're all in this together.

I've heard it said many times that nature teaches us, and this feeling of oneness, of togetherness, of belonging tonight, is bittersweet, as it also brings back how physically, socially, and culturally isolated we were in pandemic times.

But I feel ready to surrender my lasting grief over Anouk's grief. And to release mine, too, to the lack of light and to the abundance of jest, to the waggishness of our people. It's been obvious, and I should know this: Light responds to light.

Dispatches from Recovery

2024

I don't need all my life to write. I don't need all the time in the world. Come to think of it, I don't even need all of me or all of her, the woman whose manuscript has turned limp from Charleston humidity. I need, simply, to offset the two seconds that are too soon or too late. So I ask the man I call Stephen, "Do you have two seconds to spare?"

He's on his feet before I can explain what I need the two seconds for.

"I wrote something in my sketchbook," I tell him. It is the new beginning of the travel essay that was due the week I was rushed to the emergency room.

"Of course," he says, already walking to the back of the house, where the writing studio is. I follow. At the desk, he presses on keys and a light awakens and bathes us in a cool, high-energy blue. I wince and turn away—my eyes and nerves equally sensitive and easy to overwhelm. Still looking away, I crack the sketchbook open and begin to read aloud. He types. I read some more. The sound of keys clicking brings a familiarity that comforts. My shoulders peel away from my ears. I read; he types. He gives me more than the two seconds I asked for. I give myself more than what I said I'd try to give: just a sentence. This realization is in itself a reward, like I've been let in from the cold and handed a blanket. The cold, of course, is my fear of being a failure. And the blanket, well, it is the opportunity I suppose the woman

I used to be was prone to take for granted: the opportunity to do something for myself and with someone.

Warmed by my presence, the presence of someone who cares, and the sound of words streaming from my very mouth, I turn sheepishly toward the computer screen. Squinting and studying what it is I had allowed myself to do, I smile at a block of text hanging in the middle of a digital document, where it waits until I'm ready to try again.

19

Mango Trees Are for Lovers

"Mango trees are for lovers," today's tour guide tells us. And this is another way I know that Palawan is a part of my recovery story; that besides Manila, or my parents, there are other arteries by which I can remain connected to the heart that is home.

In Palawan, where the export of local mangoes is outlawed and every tree, especially the mango tree, is so prized, a couple can get married at city hall for the small fee of planting a mango sapling. On this same peninsula, a person defacing a tree, especially a mango tree, in artistic or obscene ways can face up to fifty years in prison. Nature is queen here, and whoever dares blemish her, the local community and their lawmakers believe, deserves to spend the majority of their days behind bars. Here, it is clear that there is no such thing as wilderness, that the distinction between humans and nature is a construct, and that this construct disconnects us from each other and the land. Palaweños are, truly, my people. We are sweet and severe in the same ways. It's not been easy to find Filipinos and Filipino Americans as annoyingly eco-conscious as I am, and today I feel, yet again, like I belong somewhere.

When I was eleven, my father came back for me—but only for a day. He got word of a hiking and tree-planting trip, because perhaps for once he read a parent newsletter and decided to participate in my life.

My mother saw me as something like investment property, and she saw my father just as an accessory to a childhood that had taken shape in the vestiges of his old dreams and the sidelines of his new ones. He took this new role seriously. He paid very little mind to my schooling and all other activities related to my care and tending. He was trying hard at reinstituting himself as a business figure in the rising tiger economy, which, like him, never quite roared. At the same time, he was fulfilling the job description my mother wrote for him. An easy pass if there ever was one. She wanted him out of our lives. He obliged.

He had two tasks, or should I say, two skills, remaining after his departure and his great fall of 1991. Those two things were to boast and to garner pity. How much of this dichotomized truth is a part of the postcolonial psyche, of indoctrinated and then internalized shame, I do not know to a T and can only suspect. How much of my father's case should be ascribed to the fact that upward mobility in a thrice-colonized country is beyond anyone's reality and imagination? It will only ever be a supposition. But I do know that these two things were the reasons behind his choice to chaperone a school trip three years after he abandoned me—three years after he left me crying and pleading for his stead at the top of our stairs. On the hike, he could temporarily resurrect a former handsome reputation that had to do with his success as a man who had a way with plants. He found glory, and by that I mean the confidence and venture capital of a Saudi prince, when, in the 1970s, he invented a system for growing cucumbers in the Arabian desert. Before there was #hotplantdads, there was my own dad planting Holland Hothouse cucumbers in the heat of the Gulf.

I'm nearing the age that my father was when I was born, and my daughter is now the age that I was on that hike. Children mark their parents' years not by their mothers' and fathers' milestones but by their own, and so my appraisals of him mostly took place between my day of birth and the day he reappeared like an apparition lost between helms. The verdict:

I felt ignored by him all day, which speaks for the rest of my life. He loved me, still does. But he was so consumed by his fear of failure, or of people finding out that he had already fallen, or more still, a fear of his life's definition by the simultaneous falling and people's finding out. And so he distracted them from the fact. He was very good. The decoys he made didn't much work on me as well as they did on oglers of all ages, all on the other side of the shiny mirror of his person. Perhaps that was his real skill: to make you see your likeness in him. On the trip that again felt like an abandonment, Papa made himself like everyone we went with. He taught like my teachers. He asked questions as my classmates did. He even feigned a kind of fall not long after someone else tripped on a rock. When someone helped him up, it was a perfect opportunity for him to give thanks, with a firm handhold and sustained eye contact. He told people that they were good at digging, that they wore the right boots, that they had properly spaced out the seedlings we had transported by backpack and knapsack.

Thinking about it now, maybe his tricks did work on me somehow. Maybe I believed he loved the environment because I loved it, and maybe my love of it is progeny of a more supernatural or astral keeper. Nobody in my family reads books either, so it seems like I'm just a fleck in space, not lost but held between cosmic forces set to see me grow. My birth parents were more of surrogates for the stars in the sky and the wind that made the water wave. It's freeing to think of it like that, like I can find myself in things that aren't so obvious. That there's something to find and that is seeking me back. *Light responds to light.*

I'll never age out of this yearning, and to know that something older than this republic, its laws, its colonizers, its customs, its newer iterations is coming for me and coming through me from light-years ago is to know that although we may be but dust, we are important dust. There is neither a need to boast nor to be pitied. I wish my father knew this. This wish is my love for him. This theory assuages even past miseries, that when I was given to adoption, I was really just being lent; that even when I was "undocumented," my identity was written somewhere in some magic ink that is the only ink the mango trees here may be labeled with. The triumph here, or anywhere, is in the believing.

Papa mimed how tall the trees would grow and how much sprawl they could cover. He told us we were providing shade to future hikers and homes to mammals and birds. Annoyed as I was with him, he made me love nature more with his speechifying. I believed I was affecting good, that I was an agent of some positive change. His make-believe had some usefulness to it, I guess. That doesn't mean it wasn't hurtful.

My classmates thought him a scientist, and he didn't correct them (he was an engineer). My teachers called him "Engineer Sir," and he didn't stop them (he was no longer practicing). He told them about loggers destroying our rainforests, and I just about rolled my eyes so far I could see my brain. He was always giving half stories. *He* was a logger, until he wasn't. Before he planted cucumbers and performed successive miracles in the desert, he could only find work under import/export companies that ravaged our islands and employed men with mouths to feed. He had always respected nature, like I did, and do, which was rare in our immediate and extended families—both of which had held fast to postwar consumerism. They were absorbed into the blur of excesses, *surpluses*, given us by foreigners: American, Chinese, Japanese, Saudi, emirate—name it. It was impossible to escape this new kind of colonialism, the kind that makes you want to love and hoard everything that obscures a purer, more ancestral knowledge of self. We took the plastic that they gave us. We became Levi's, Nike, Toshiba, rhinoplasty. I want to believe that my father loved trees—until he had to love his first wife and first children more and cut the trees down. He had to, if he was going to afford to give them plastic. It's an immigrant story, after all, and it's bound to have a trade-off. A loss for every gain.

Of all his children, then and now, I am the only one to care about nature, and I attribute it to being the youngest (a millennial) and to '90s shows like *Captain Planet* as well to the leftovers that he gave me. And so, when the trip became Our Trip, I expected it to be, in fact, about us—not solely about him. I spent most of that day digging and planting, my nails caked in dirt by the end, and he spent it making a spectacle of himself. He had a sprightly mustache that aided and abetted this mission. He was proud of how hard I had worked, or so he said at some point, but what I wanted—needed—was to be company, to be shoulder to shoulder with someone in their doing and their waiting.

Of course now, in this tour van, as we are learning about mango trees and the romances they support, I am shoulder to shoulder with someone whose doing and waiting I share and witness daily. And he is not one for fanfare, not one with a need to be a star. He's never used our woes, financial or professional or otherwise, as some kind of ploy. I never feel indebted to him and neither do I ever feel like he owes me. For all the analytic efforts I gave toward the careful consideration of marrying a white man whose settler-colonist ancestors continue to own the same parcel in South Carolina, it was the very knowable truth of his infinite and sincere humility and the feeling I still get that he needs me never but wants me always that caused me to say, "Okay, fine, Stephen. I'll date you."

Maybe what I'm thinking about here now, actually, is reclamation. I came home to the Philippines to claim back abstract matter, like time and cultural proximity and joyful associations to my country, for myself and for my child. I am here to reassert a right to be nothing, not for anybody, and to be something, someone, only on my own terms. My parents always needed me for something. My mother canvassed material resources from me. My father wanted and wanted and wanted, and still wants, emotional petting. There's always talk everywhere now about having boundaries, and I'm glad for it. What I'm not glad about is the clapback and backlash. "You should be grateful," they tell us. And I can say back, "No, *you* should be grateful."

I love my parents forever, forward and backward in time, but I don't make myself available to them now because, like the economies that have either thwarted my growth or forced it "exponentially," they've been extractive. Both have never matured slowly but surely like a mango tree. But I still can. When the tour guide, who is Batak, finishes his spiel about containing mango weevils and how the Palawan mango is the sweetest in the archipelago because it's grown in soil enriched by uninterrupted natural processes, biodiversity, and Palauan, Batak, and Tagbanua care, I ask what he knows of mango tree care. It's simple, he says: "Plenty water, plenty sun, and, people always forget, plenty of pruning."

"Mango trees are for lovers," I remember him saying just earlier. And it's true. They remind us that sweet fruit is born from trees that have received proper care, get lots of nourishment, and like all else, prosper when cut off from dead or dying branches, flourish in their existence as living things sufficient unto themselves. I wish we had planted mangoes on that long-ago hike. Maybe we did; I don't recall exactly what saplings and seedlings we'd brought with us. But here's what I do remember: Descending from the bald top of the mountain, Papa and I walked side by side for a short time. I had our water bottles, among other things, in my backpack. I could already tell from the way he gulped down his share of our water that he needed more—some of mine, that is. I unscrewed the top to my bottle before he supped up the rest of his and drank to my heart's content, leaving him none. I could have felt cruel, and maybe I did. Like the sun and the rain, there's a time for everything, even selfishness. So I hope now that I should never thirst for my own daughter's share of water, never let the earth under her leach dry, never take nutrient away from her growing and from the prospect of sweetness, of golden fruit in the shape of a heart.

Dispatches from Recovery

2024

What is this feeling? What is this tickle spreading from my throat to my arms? This is the third, maybe fourth, time we've sat like this, me reciting what I wrote in my sketchbook and him asking me to slow down a little because he's not the fastest typist in the world. Why am I unbothered to catch him biting his nails to nothing or adjusting himself in his pants while he types? And why the hell am I watching him do it? I can't stop looking at his crotch for chrissakes! What the fuck is happening and why do I like it?

"What do you think?" he says.

WHAT-WHAT, what do you mean?! *"Not thinking anything!" I say, pretending to search for a word in my thesaurus, my closest confidant of late and so far the only remedy to my poor word recall.*

"So, leave it like that? Is that how you want it?" he says, pointing at the line breaks between paragraphs.

I turn my head to the computer screen he's dimmed for my comfort, turning so fast that I invite a dizzy spell. I bring my hand and the thesaurus over my eyes and peep and say, "Yes, the line breaks are good, but don't add quotation marks because I just don't trust that what I'm recalling is verbatim."

"I could double-check and listen to your tapes again," he offers.

"No, that's too much work for now," I say. "Thank you for—"

Before I can begin listing all the things he does for me and I'm grateful for, I am staring at his crotch again, and he catches me. And he's leaning forward before I can excuse myself, and the next thing I know is we are on the old, rickety sofa in the writing studio, breathing on each other, my brain's reward system suddenly located and activated, and all there is to think about, whether it's regarding this or him or the travel essay or the line breaks or the fact that I'm slowly but surely writing again, is that I am here, in this world, with still so much earthly and human beauty left to see and know and be confounded or delighted or even be irked by.

20

Paper Airplane

We are, it turns out, people who make friends on vacation:

Filipino Australian backpacking sisters who take great photos of us and of our food.

Seattle-based Filipino American retirees and their adult son who invite us to winter with them.

Another Filipino family from Australia, the teenage son moodier than the daughter; we never see him in the pool or the lounge.

Two English girls from the Cotswolds, cousins if I'm remembering correctly, who hitched a boat ride with us on snorkeling day.

The lone Serbian who asks me to air-drop my videos because they're less pixelated, more high-definition than his.

A returnee from Dubai who advises Stephen to find a job at an international school here, who keeps saying, "Good job, good pay, car and condo included. You could take your wife home."

In turns, we eat with these friends, drink beer with them while we hang our legs over the pool's edge, and swap seats with them when one of us is carsick and needs to sit shotgun in the van. We swap stories too: comings and goings. They've all been back several times over the years. For some, they've returned often but just before the pandemic. They all still believe that there is no place like home, that there's more beauty left to experience here. It is, after all, an archipelago of more than seven thousand islands. When the information finally leaks and they learn that not only is this Anouk's first time in the Philippines but also my first time back in twenty years, they each in their own way conjure an atmosphere of compassion and care.

One of the mothers buys us calamari as a dinner appetizer; the other mother helps me find a snorkeling mask that fits Anouk's narrow face. "Has to fit, you know? Has to be snug."

When we forget to take more cash from the hotel safe, the dad from Seattle loans us bills, tells us not to worry about it. The girls from the Cotswolds, after every snorkeling stop, ask Anouk to describe the sea life she saw, which fish is her favorite. "Me too," they say, "me too."

The Aussie sisters share their edible souvenirs with us: hopia, buko pandan, pastillas. They call me "ate." They braid Anouk's hair. She likes that they include her, cuddle her in when they're browsing outfits online. She enjoys teetering into their teendom and young adulthood, as long as she feels like Mom's right there, still within reach. She's gotten much bigger, leggier since quarantine, her looks fitting neatly into the precociousness and wisdom she's always had. The Aussie sisters and the Aussie mom and the Seattle-based couple say they've never met such a good kid, a kid who can hang.

"A kid like this deserves the world," the dad from Seattle says. "Give her everything."

Stephen and I exchange knowing looks.

We've known them for a total of only four days, but, at least here, at least for us, four days is long enough to, on a whim, get tattoos with two of them while we wait out the rain. "You and I could get it," I tell Anouk. "It's just henna."

It's our last island-hopping stop, on Cowrie Island, and the rain has finally decided to come down. "The rain. I know this rain. It's the rain that I know," I said when we arrived, my voice captured on video as I recorded our deboard on this last stop on a snorkeling excursion. It's the only video I don't share with the Serbian. I keep it for myself.

The last time I saw my mother happy, she was dancing tits-out in this rain. So ridiculous and, for once, so free. It's what I'm thinking about now, seated in this plastic chair in the middle of a nipa hut housing a henna tattoo artist and his basket of blues, greens, and blacks.

I know this rain. It's the rain that I know. A cleansing, a blessing. On some islands they say that it comes down when werehorses and such creatures wed. On other islands, the belief is that it's brought on by someone pitchy or off-key, a reflection of how everything here comes back, if not to food, to singing. There is, in fact, singing. On the opposite hedge of this narrow and long island, a woman sings a Regine Velasquez hit into a karaoke microphone attached to a portable speaker they had packed with their picnic. What can I say? It's who we are. Practical with a touch of flair.

As the Aussie sisters' teddy bears and Anouk's panda dry on their skin, I get inked on my left clavicle: a paper airplane cruising through the sky from a point of departure in the vicinity of my heart. A static sound breaks through the pelting as the woman with the karaoke selects a new song. The whole of the island cringes. When she begins again, my paper airplane is done. When her song ends, the rain does too.

Anouk inspects my new accessory. "I love it, Mama," she says. "You like mine?"

I bring my nose close to her panda's nose. For a second, she's as young as she was when she first asked to come here, that evening in the tub. "What a silly guy, like you. I like him."

"I like him too," she says. "I like everything here." She continues, with a lingering of her younger self. "Everything here is beautiful . . . pacifically [specifically] after the rain."

~

There is a European woman, maybe German, maybe Dutch, fretting about butter at the pastry end of the breakfast buffet. She has broken a butter dish and blames it on how cold to the touch the ceramic dish is. "So cold!" she yells.

Her ponytail bounces as she berates the server. He explains that it's a hot day today and the added humidity from the steaming vats and chafing dishes don't help in keeping the squares of precut butter from melting. They freeze the dishes before breakfast service for this reason. As he says this, in a kind and endearing and, in my opinion, too submissive way that makes his voice lilt, she reaches for another butter dish. As though it were supercharged and voltaic, she flings it upon touch. The dish shatters. Shards rocket every way. The little square of butter balances on what's left of the hearty middle of the little plate, a melty hexahedron, a die in her game. A toddler sucking on bread watches the butter's edges thaw as the woman pivots on her heels and walks away, rambling, hands frantic in the air.

Out of curiosity, I push my chair back and begin walking to the pastry stand to see just how cold "so cold" is. Anouk's chest rises. I roll my eyes. *C'mon.* Halfway to the pastries, a piece of ceramic crunches under my clunky orthopedic sandals. I reach to pluck off the shard from my shoe, and on my way down the server and I almost butt heads because he's trying to reach for the same shard I'm reaching for. We're both crouched down. I take it as an opportunity to make conversation. We're sweeping ceramic pieces on terra-cotta tiles with the backs of our hands, fast to outpace the other, and he says, "Madam, please, no. I do it."

I respond in Tagalog and tell him that it's fine, I'm happy to help.

"Ay Tagalog!" he says, surprised that a balayage blonde balikbayan speaks the national and local tongue. He smiles, eyes cast back down, careful still to not cross some line.

I hand him my collection of shards, and notice he is still wary of eye contact. So, I say, in Tagalog, "Gusto mo awayin ko siya?"

He looks up, fast. Now we are eye to eye. "Ha, Madam?!" He's shocked I've just offered to fight the European woman on his behalf.

"English pa, kaya ko. Ano? Gusto mo? Awayin ko? Paduguin ko yung tenga?"

He and his fellow servers ogle, stunned by my fighter spirit and eagerness to cross the woman. It *is* early in the day. I can see in their wrinkled foreheads and how their mouths hang open just how petrified they are of a possible bout. Imagine: two guests yelling about butter at the breakfast buffet.

I say, "Pakshit," a Filipinization of "fuck" and "shit," and I do it with the sultry eyes of a teleserye villain about to disrupt a protagonist's wedding. When I punctuate my mini performance with a dramatic hair flip, they understand that I'm joking, that I won't really cuss out the woman and make her ears bleed with my crass tongue. I am the dirty mouth in our family of three, that's long been established, but I'm not belligerent, well, not always and certainly not on vacation, not even when a white woman has mistreated a kababayan on our own land. She doesn't deserve my cusses, but the servers, my countrymen, deserve my jokes.

The serving crew, about four of them, breaks out in laughter. Some hide their giggles behind a plastic serving tray or sweaty water pitcher. The woman turns her head to us, and she knows what's the matter. For fun, I give her the side-eye. I hold it. It's long. She shields her face from my stare by pressing down on her tennis visor. Luxury vacation is about comfort, and so I give her none.

When I'm back on my feet, I reach out my hand to the servers to introduce myself. They hesitate before reaching back. I learn their names one by one, and they learn mine, and they ask me if I'm from America or Australia or England. I give the elevator-pitch version of the story: I'm here after twenty years in the United States. And when they hear "twenty," the mood is somber again, but only momentarily. One asks if I'd like a coffee refill; another asks if I've tried the mango and black sesame suman. I take whatever they offer me, my hands and forearms filling fast with hot and cold dishes. In America, I waited tables to put myself through college and to put Anouk through preschool and to pay for my mother's supposed medical bills. They get a sense of this experience by the way I've stacked the plates. *Arm me with another*, a click of the tongue and a boastful flick of my hand says.

Suman, ensaymada, kutsinta.

Danggit, dilis.

Garlic rice.

I walk my loot back to our table. Mikky, the European woman's prey, walks with me and asks who it is I am traveling with. When I point with my pursed lips to my girl with similar hips and similar buck teeth, and to Ted Lasso in the fishing hat, Mikky waves two fingers to them and, whether he's seen the hit comedy or not, says—appropriately, or appropriatingly, either way it's a gotcha—"Howdy!"

The villa is cool and fragrant upon our return from the day's excursions. Beds have been turned down, towels replaced, and the kalachuchi flowers on our nightstands and vanity refreshed. I've not been this pampered since my wedding day and the only time I've soaked in a Jacuzzi bubbling with signature-collection soap and fragranced with cut flowers during an early-career book tour stop in my publisher's base city, the five-star touches a splurge rewarded to me for my first book's mild but cherished success. *I'm on vacation,* I think to myself, and turn the tap at the mouth of the egg-shaped tub.

The world's water problems are always top of mind for me, even after leaving my water-focused NGO job, so I shake my head and sigh out my thoughts to prepare myself for some indulgence. I slide into the fat foam and warm water, tickled by the bubbles and my learning to relax. And then, another sigh. Apart from feeling the hug of water around me, I feel the sharp contrast between making friends with fellow Filipino returnees and making friends with hotel staff. Whatever the former, myself included, have brought in terms of Aussie and American dollars and British pounds complicates dynamics at this resort. My new friendship with one differs from my new friendship with the other, glaringly and palpably so. I've chosen to befriend both but, needless to say, my "hard work" in America affords me the choice of who to engage with, and how. Having been in the United States for twenty years has allowed me time, space, and material and social resources that have altogether shown me how classist my own upbringing was, despite how loudly and painfully my stomach growled from hunger many nights of living under my mother's roof.

Like the twin gratitude and dismay I feel toward America, in tandem are my gratitude for being back in my motherland and my dismay over how social stratification, like my mother's influence, continues to tentacle through this place. In America, the divides are mainly drawn up by race, class, doctrine, and geography. In the Philippines, it's the invented rankings we inherited from the Spanish—family prestige, rungs of Westernization, and generational land ownership—that all but dictate who belongs where and with whom. Being comfortable in the Philippines has long had something to do with how close you were to the Spanish colonizing line, and later it also meant proximity to Americanness or Australianism or Chinese money or emirati investment—name any foreign influence. Here I am, returning to my home country after two decades, thirsting for cultural connection and millennialese authenticity, confined, no matter what, in a world shadowed by imperialism's lasting, pervading ramifications.

But so wordy, is it not? As if Mikky would care to listen, as if he had the time to hear me explain that while I've crossed oceans, my real life in the home I've built is rarely a breeze. *America!* Those we leave behind will say, believing we've "made it" to the other side and remaining oblivious to hardships, systemic and personal, we endure abroad. I lean back and rest my neck on the towel the hotel staff have preemptively rolled up for this very use and very kind of moment, and I tempt myself to think that none of it matters anyway. What good is my explaining? It isn't like I can show up at the breakfast buffet tomorrow morning armed with good-sense guilt and my speechifying. But I can believe, at least while this bathwater is still warm, I've already crossed an ocean by making fun of that European woman. I've already bridged some divide with my humor and bilingualism. Like I did when considering the resort-goers at Jamaica's Secrets, I kick the water at my feet out of frustration. *I try,* I tell myself. What matters is that I try.

Frustration is a good sign because it means altruism, that you allowed your thoughts to emerge, that you own your thoughts at all. It's what I tell myself because it's what I'd tell Anouk. Sometimes, I believe, it does me good to be compassionate with myself as I am with her. The understanding my child deserves? I deserve it too. I gently soap around the henna paper airplane on my chest and talk to myself again, this time like Stephen does when consoling a good student emotionally, mentally demolished by an atypical low score: "I swear you already care more than the average mouth-breathing idiot. It's gonna be okay." I linger in the bath until it's tepid, hoping my attention is only ever larger than this tub and my compassion only ever hotter than this water, no matter the contradictory yet concurrent, truths I'm always bound to fly between.

Dispatches from Recovery

2024

There are good days and bad days and worse days.

Some days I'm well enough to paint watercolors of images I have in my head: a beach, a cape, a parade. On these good days, I can also take a shower (independently, in fact), check Anouk's homework, and write a letter to a person I'm happy to address as friend.

On the bad days, I'm so fatigued and nauseated that the extent of what I can do is change into clean sweatpants (again, independently) and read a poem from a book Erin, another friend of mine, sent. The rest of the day is spent napping, icing my head, or closing my eyes while I imagine myself mobile and traveling—the rocking, reeling feeling of being waist-deep in ocean water and wading toward a sleepy shoal—or swinging in a hammock somewhere, with memories from my past, from before the rupture in my brain, as heirlooms of hope and happiness from my old self to my new self in this now time.

Then there are strings of mortifyingly painful hours, horrifying nights, when the curtains close all around me, and I am trapped in the very mind asking and willing me to trust. Trust that the pain has an end, and the confusion too. Or—when more curtains close between me and the moment and space I'm trying so hard to inhabit, and the end is unbelievable—instead of holding fast to the present, I allow myself to recede deep into the heirlooms, dissociated as I may be from the now but floating calmly and confidently in a sea of long-term memories I'm grateful to have intact and I'm receiving open-handedly, open-heartedly, like opening a letter I wrote from way back when, a letter from a former self I'm also trying to befriend.

21

Perlas ng Silanganan

Every inheritance is an accord. We bequeath heirlooms to mark milestones, even celebrate them, and often at the receding borders of a bygone or passing time. When we give it, whatever it is, we know and hopefully accept that the passing of it changes it, that part of it is forever different, if not forever gone. It's how I felt when Stephen proposed to me with a pearl ring given to him by his mother and given to her by her sister, who'd passed away.

I was surprised by when and how Stephen proposed, sly and sweet and sunset-timed, in an open field next to a peach farm. But I was not surprised that the moment came, finally, because we'd been talking about marriage for a year. We were too young, we both agreed. But unmarried, I would stay undocumented. And while marriage is never the cure for anything, it was at least a way to keep me from further injury, from the unremitting hazards and instability of being without a "valid" identity as defined by the state. So the decision to get married was less curative, more preventive. And again, I was young. I had so much ahead of me that could still be taken from me by the "status."

That evening, bathed in golden light, I said yes, and when he slid the dainty gold band, a pearl set between two twinkles of mini diamanté, onto my finger, what we were really doing was dressing me for a future not yet with us but that we fully expected to arrive. I was going to become, on paper, American. I was going to have the protections that he had.

The ring fit. Perfectly. There was no fidgeting with it. It slid right on just as quickly as an unfamiliar smugness came upon Stephen's face, a look I trusted simply because I was grinning in the same way, like we had a plan, some shared foresight, some politics not always conveniently matching with the aesthetics of the life we were beginning to make. We were marrying; he was re-Southerning as I was becoming American. People had started to gift us monogrammed gingham. And yet none of the conventions were going to hold, *that* we knew, and this knowledge was worth every giggle and snicker under that sherbet sky, the tall pampas and purple cattail blurring the edges of us, as in a watercolor painting.

But, so it goes, the ring was an inheritance, an understanding. It was being changed the moment it started to warm on my hand. Stephen was thrilled that a pearl passed from one generation to another in a farming family hailing from settler-colonists would find its way to the dainty fingers of a dancer, a writer, an artist from the Pearl of the Orient Seas. That the same young lady would have the strong legs and stance of a futbolera. We didn't yet know the specifics of the reverse migration of the pearl, but we could already feel its power. The ring—the pearl—would find its way back to the very sea from which it was most probably harvested, to Palawan, where pearls of up to fourteen pounds have been found.

On the same evening, on our walk back from the field, he took something from his pocket, something balled up like a tissue holding a child's baby tooth. I thought he was giving me something like that, a gag gift, and that it was supposed to be funny when all I could take it for was gross. But within seconds, when the ball started to unravel in his hand, it began to show its preciousness: unwrinkled fabric the same color and sheen as the pearl, powder-blue scalloped stitching on the hem, more crisscrossing of pastel threads that together formed a tiny farmer, a tinier carabao, hints of a rice field, a hut, two coconut trees, and these words:

Sweetheart

Manila

1945

It was the embroidered handkerchief his paternal grandfather had custom-made for his grandmother in the last year of the Second World War, when he was on his second deployment as an army chaplain and photographer. He was first in Germany, and when Japan's fury could not be contained in our islands, he was among tens of thousands of American soldiers sent by one empire to vanquish another. It was one slaughter after the other. Camps and weapons were built by both sides, of every kind and for every gruesome purpose. The man never fired a gun. He photographed the many violences.

At times, as I discovered when I digitized images from old negatives he had kept in a box, he photographed children playing in destruction, cows grazing ravaged land, plants sprouting in cracks formed by explosives. With his per diem, Granddad, as Stephen called him, paid for a hand-embroidered silk from a shop somehow still standing among the ruins of what would painfully, slowly grow back into a city that would birth me two generations thereafter. I don't know if he had it made because he was hopeful for his life, that he would see his sweetheart again, or that he himself would do the dramatic reveal from his pocket. Or if he meant to keep it balled up and stuffed in his green uniform should he be found blasted or slashed or decapitated: proof of a shortened life nonetheless made full by love. Historically, American battles in my homeland are considered the United States' worst military defeat because of the sheer numbers. No tally is perfect or official, but every tally ever attempted accounts, or recounts, a horrifying figure.

Granddad survived. He went home to his sweetheart, a woman I only got to know when the sweetness in her heart had been snuffed out by old age. But that she would give Stephen the gift and instruct him to pass it on to its new and rightful owner just about eclipsed the moods that swung about erratically after her beloved's death. The gesture was mostly symbolic—my country remains systemically ruined, naturally depleted, and bound by one-sided treaties. It was, like our marriage, not a cure but a prevention. It would not, on its own, turn things right side up but only show acceptance that there was—is—a right side. It was an act out of step with history, more in step with the times, and dancing along the way, further and further from the impolitic alternative, which is to keep what to one never belonged, and by this I mean less the actual kerchief and more the meaning of art and artifact, especially in times of war. For the centuries Stephen's paternal side had spent in church work, it was perhaps, in my opinion, the most Christian, or Christlike, thing they'd done.

I always liked the old man. He never looked at me the way some other relatives looked at me and never used an air or a disposition or even gentility to hold me at arm's length, knowing what he knew about me. When we first met, he held my hand right away and pulled me close to whisper to my ear, "This one's a good one." There was half a breath between the handhold and the whisper, an unspoken preface that, sure, Stephen was the least obvious choice for a partner. Why would I ever leave my beloved New York for this Southern boy? But he said those words with a knowing look, like when someone's light eyes turn deeper in their color and you can see into them. Like the smugness on Stephen's face the night of our engagement, it was a look I trusted quickly and because the sentiment behind it was something I already shared. Time had already done its job. What our souls knew, our consciousness was already grasping. If we were nervous at all about the prospect that lay before us, it was because we cared and could already feel the weight of the influence at hand.

What I found surprising was how Granddad had taste. He liked to dress, the pictures show. Spiffy in tailored suits that ran forever down his long body, another semblance between him and his grandson, another petty but welcome betrayal, I thought, of their ruralness and Southernness and Americanness. And the colors he chose for the kerchief, the satin he selected, the placement of the simple stitches: very much unlike ruffled embroidery selections at Southern gift shoppes (yes, with the double *p* and the *e*—that kind), very much something Stephen would buy for me now. The kerchief was a kerchief, after all—it takes a tasteful person to even know what it is. Its most striking feature was and continues to be its plainness, a simplicity lending so much to a way with grace, a way that I'm attracted to when I browse leather notebooks or ecru earthenware or everyday gold jewelry. Or the black-and-white shotgun house I won with my kindness. Like now, like in this pearl emporium that is the last stop on our last Palawan tour, where I'm looking for inexpensive earrings to bring back to friends and cousins and in-laws and matching rings for me and Anouk. Inevitably, I am thinking about my original pearl and its bequeathal's original and withstanding meaning. I am thinking of how pearls are made from debris caught in an oyster: trash to treasure. I am thinking of how history can be cruel, and how, in its effort to foil, time gives us coincidences, concurrences, and correlations. Joan Didion said that we tell ourselves stories in order to live. And maybe with all the pain that precedes my and Stephen's union, all the weight of his country's and my country's intertwining, all the wounds that have come from one or the other's attempt at untangling, I tell myself these stories not to pacify but to allay the pressure to do what's right, the pressure that no one but myself places on me. I want to recover, and I want the same for my country. I also want it for my love and for his country.

And maybe this is what it means for me to be Filipino American. I don't go to protests and sign petitions and call my representatives and write all there is to write because I hate my birth and adopted countries. I do it all because, as with anything touched by love and formed in truth, it is worth evading shrapnel for on your way to the battlefield—to find the sole craftsperson and pay for what their hands can make, be it a picture to hang or a hat to don or a kerchief to catch your laughs or your coughs or your tears—and you believe that to undo destruction, to re-create order, like street performers in the Ukraine and fashion designers making gowns from deadstock in the Anthropocene, a belief in goodness and beauty helps get us there.

I'm thankful that Granddad was one of not so many who made it back, that he wasn't one of 150 wrapped in dynamite here in Puerto Princesa or one of thousands more machine-gunned or bayoneted in Manila, Batanes, too many elsewheres. I do wish he could have commissioned the textile art in something other than the context of war, like how my purchasing heirloom jewelry for Anouk sits in the middle of a lovely two-week vacation. The Philippines, since a generation after the war, became a place of government corruption, poverty, flash floods, deeply eroded soil, shifts in rainfall, even droughts. Irreversible damage left and right, like the body that carries trauma at the cellular level, its chromosomal telomeres altered in length, forever changed and encumbered by what it's endured. Colonialism's impacts. But Palawan and its Indigenous keepers and their allies remain. Although not completely spared by storms, the peninsula makes evident that we can choose regeneration where and when available, opt out of garbage, and break from pattern. I won't resolve everything in my lifetime, and there aren't enough pearls in the ocean and in this mart to democratize ownership and distribution of them. But I have these four in my hands, a black pearl and a white pearl on each of the matching rings I bargained for, a skill I'm glad to have not lost over two decades with a memory like that of riding a bike headed home. I still got game. My bargaining is a spectacle to no one but my two. What an opportunity to show this side of me, what a chance to be beheld.

The black and white pearls touch but they do not merge. They float on the finger from two ends of a thin and braided wire. They are nimble around each other, like the feet that tread lightly but surely and make right what is in their path.

Everything is still analog here at the emporium. I hand over the cash, and a receipt and customs form are written out with a ballpoint pen. Anouk wants to wear her ring right away. We shake our heads at an offer of an iridescent cardboard box. I anchor my ring on a pinkie. I place hers in the crook of her hand, for her to slide on her own finger. We are already refusing garbage, already breaking pattern. Someone once wrote a review of my first book: "You are chosen. You are breaking generational curses." I don't usually look at reviews but that particular one was destined to be found. I read it off my phone, my ring finger curling around the device. The pearl engagement ring was already tight on me eight years after I received it. And it won't be long until I pass it on.

Dispatches from Recovery

2024

I am back to spelling my name, this time assisted by the girl who recently went from smelling like a classroom to smelling of cool cucumber, white tea, and a touch of jasmine. A scent so familiar because, it turns out, it is my scent—the same fragrance Stephen says lingers in his memory from our college years and lingers on because, apparently, I am one of those diehards who buy select beauty products in bulk as a work-around against that cruel act that cosmetic manufacturers habitually commit: discontinuation. (And isn't that what I'm fighting against here? Isn't that the particular brand of entropy I'm raising a middle finger to? In my writing, my recuperating, my clutching at my thesaurus, the way I say necessary lies to the girl about what I know and what I recall?) The girl likes to raid my closet, at first for tops and pullovers and of late for perfume I lucked upon, Stephen says, on one of my monthly hunts through T.J. Maxx, a land he jokes is where I really come alive because there my penny-pinching and nostalgia and vanity can coexist.

The girl who dresses like me and now smells like me sits to my right, nodding as the grief therapist gives us this week's joint homework. We are, we are told, to spell each other's names using descriptors. As an example, the therapist spells her own name:

T—terrific
R—righteous

A—admirable

C—comfortable

Y—yellow—my favorite color!

All horrible words, *I thought. And, as I'm guessing from her attempt at not laughing and her lip bite and her sitting on her hands, the girl thinks so too. The therapist logs off and our session ends, and as soon as the screen blinks to black, the girl and I are rolling off the couch, catching our breaths between roiling, curdling, snorting laughs.* How boring and asinine, *we both clearly think! For a therapist, the woman sure has zero training in self-awareness—or the English language! Was she meaning to describe herself or a pair of bedroom slippers?* Terrific! Comfortable! Yellow! *There has to be some way to bar a person from acquiring a therapist license when the best they can do for capturing their sense of self is to use vocabulary straight from a kindergarten teacher's dollar-store sticker book!*

But the girl and I are united by a sense of duty—too bad neither of our names have the letter D. *When the hilarity wears off, to the page we go. I begin to spell out who she is one letter at a time, and she begins, elbow and forearm shielding her paper like it's a math test and I'm a cheating schoolmate.*

Scribble, scribble, I finish first and read:

A—amicable, artistic, athletic, ancient soul

N—nice, natural beauty, nurturing, (everything you do is) noteworthy

O—optimistic, original, obedient (in that you're a rule follower when it counts for the common good)

U—unique, understanding, uplifting, upright

K—kind, knowledgeable, keen-eyed, karmic, a keeper

I've made her smile, an expression she keeps as she takes a long breath in. It's her turn to read. Her list, as I can now see, is longer, fuller. She reads off words for each letter keenly (keen-eyed, as I told you), and I feel how much more intention she's pumped into the activity and how much more assurance and consoling she's sourcing from it.

C—caring, compassionate, creative

I—intelligent, interesting, introspective, intuitive

I remember now. I taught her letters not long ago, helping her progress in first-grade reading and writing by setting up her days so that she never went to bed without having read a thing, no matter the size of the tantrum she threw or the infernal contortions her body made when she made a fuss. I was her pandemic lockdown e-learning tutor, both of us often in tears because it was lonely to stare at a screen and lonelier still not to. When school reopened, after all the scowling and digressions and excuses, she was thankful to know her diphthongs and silent letters. Suddenly, in class she had a forte. And today, apparently, marks when the pupil surpasses the instructor. She puts her lexical prowess, and knowing of me, on display. I fall silent, as the k *in* knowing *is there but silent.*

N—nice, nurturing, natural beauty

Save for the arrangement of words, we do, in fact, resemble each other. We, because it is what we know love to be, mirror each other's light.

E—educated, empathetic, eloquent

As she reads, I think of how every word she uses to describe me also applies to her. We take pride in our abilities to think, to feel, to speak . . . even when a brain injury threatens the existence or dependability of such traits, full is the tank that holds and impermeable are the love and courage that protect. I am a den inhabited by my two wolves, they who come crying back when I howl, WHO.

L—loving, loyal, lucky

L—lovable, lighthearted

E—encouraging, even-tempered, emotional

Every letter, every word plucks me back from the places in my mind. Every letter, every word awakens me to myself. I watch her lips move—lips that sure do look like mine, her teeth too. She's right here. I'm right here. This is it. No matter the number, vastness, quirks, or perks of any other universes, it is in this one where we share a last name, a home address, a limp, a wardrobe, a fragrance, a sense of humor, a critical eye when it comes to appraising just about anything and anyone, an addiction to hard work and most forms of sugar, and a lanky, athletic-although-sometimes-ponderous Hugh Grant–handsome, Ted Lasso–wholesome, Pokémon-collecting, ice-cream-and-Old-Fashioned-loving man.

S—sensitive

T—tolerant of all my tantrums

E—enamored by us, like we are tadpoles to hold in his hands

P—peaceful and patient and persistent and playful

H—hope of my hope and heroic in the quietest, most unobtrusive ways

E—eager to bring me back to myself and just as earnest in his bringing me back to my writing

N—nimble in his stepping here, there, everywhere he can find the pieces of me

Words, letters. They're all around. Markers for who I am, opportunities to be me. I really shouldn't fret, or at least if I do fret, I can fret over which one to embody in the moment, fret over how many choices I have for how to trace the shape of my happening, my living, my life.

22

No Plans

We've been sleeping within earshot of where sea urchins rattle their spines, where shrimp snap their backs, and while I can't say that I can hear them, I can say that because our villa sits so close to the kayak landing, even with my bad left ear, I can hear how precious the kayak operators are about all that lies beneath the water's surface. Every few moments, the wind carries over to us a kindly suggestion: *Careful where you step. Slowly, slowly, slower. Gentle paddles, gentle.*

It's a morning with no planned excursions, no activity paid for through an app. The first thing to do after yet another leisurely breakfast is to allow ourselves to be absorbed into the dewy air that meets us wherever we turn. Stephen suggested we get on the complimentary kayaks, and out to the sandbar he ventured to on our first full day. He said that while Anouk and I loved the pool, he thought it unforgivable to skip on the amenity, like how it would have been deplorable to sleep in on our only Montego Bay beach day. It was less an opinion, more a wonderment. And so, into water shoes our feet go and out the door and to the landing.

When we cross the bamboo bridge, it is clear that the mangroves, bestrewn with spindly trees, and the sandbar, paunchy and oval and rising and falling in the water like a sleeping infant's navel, are both beautiful beyond comprehension. But it is not solely this beauty, this nothing-but-ornamental beauty, that I find so affecting this morning. It's the feeling of fragility that comes upon you when you're leaving somewhere and the simultaneous feeling of being looked after, like when Stephen finds my charger under the hotel bed after I've just again looked there. Today it's kayak operators doing the double-checking, making sure we have appropriate footwear to protect us from stonefish and urchin and appropriate paddles for our heights. It's all too close to when Buki or Nancy or my cousin Jen visit and bring a craft kit and keep Anouk, shooing us out of the house for a night out. I'm inspired. I propose a creative way for romance and tell Anouk, leggy and athletic girl that she is, that today is the perfect low-tide day to get in her own kayak. And again, on vacation, it's the little things.

Our pointy, plastic vessels wade in slow.

The operator pats the air: *Slowly, slowly, slower.*

Apart from us, there's only a trio of riders already farther ahead. I sit pilot this morning, and when the fog breaks where it meets our heads, I go into a tonic state, immobilized by the sight of three brown wild horses, two adults and a foal, making their way back to another mangrove. Even Anouk is unable to say her famous words: *Ma! Mom! Look!* The operator turns to give me a thumbs-up, and I must and I do raise him one back. When we arrive at the shoal and disembark, it's the horses' hoofprints that we follow across the sand, and whichever way they lead us, there's a blue sea star or chocolate-chip one, lazy in the water, being pretty as pretty does. Where the hoofprints make a roundabout, a sea cucumber and its thousand feet crimple the sand and the seagrass, and Anouk and I bite our teeth because it's cool and it's icky.

Stephen wanders off to where he found the bluest of blue starfish a few days ago, and Anouk follows. They keep walking until they are suddenly stopped in their tracks. They stare down at what I'm sure is not nothing but likely another portal they're opening, another wrinkle in time.

The trio that preceded us is hip-deep now in water, and I can see that they've brought cast nets like the ones I learned to catch crab with in South Carolina. The tallest of them is tall because he's long and because he stands confidently, like an angler sure of a good catch today. I'm drawn to this feeling of assurance and walk to him as he pulls a knife from his waistband. He drops to his knees and shaves the sand in circular movements, fast and precise, and like he's peeling an apple from the inside. I don't notice that he also has a thin bamboo stick on him until he uses it to make one swift stabbing movement into the center of the crater he's made. When he pulls out the stick, there's a whitish tubular creature around it, like pale nylons on a slender leg.

"Kuya, squid?" I say.

"Parang squid," he responds. "Wakwak. Masarap." He rolls it off the stick just like you would a pair of tights, tears off the edge, and offers me a bite.

My eyes get big, but I don't want to offend, so I ask if I can instead help him catch another, if he could teach me how to dig them up from the sand.

By the time Anouk and Stephen make their way to where I am on the shoal, I've gotten the full (free) tutorial, and my knife skills are already a lot less shaky than at first. I'm horrible at it but so happy. I try another time just to show Anouk what I've been taught, to no avail, so I show her the kuya's catch. Her ability to speak returns, and she says, "Ma! Mom! Whoa!"

He asks if she likes calamari, and she nods. He says they're similar in taste and how they're cooked. He poses for me and with me for a few pictures, wakwak dangling from his fingers, and soon the kayak operator is calling to us, "High tide na po, mamsir."

We get in our rides and head back toward the villas. I give the sandbar many last looks. This place is officially unsubtle about its allure. The family of horses, the creatures in the shallows, the new friend, and the new (almost) skill: Palawan shows off its every ornamentation this last morning, teasing, *There's more where all that idle, pointless, trivial stuff came from.* We head to another island tonight, to Mactan, Cebu, for a festival I remember as the one and only time my father did something fun. But before we enter a time of painted masks, hand-dyed feathers, parading, and dancing, a time for reliving good memories of him, I look back this way for the sixtieth time and blow a kiss to a mound of sand already disappearing in incoming water. I wish my father wasn't always working, wasn't always speechifying. I wish he did with me many idle, pointless, trivial things. At least now, I'll know where to look again should I find myself wanting, needing something of the like. There's a shoal like the navel of a sleeping infant, rising and falling as it trusts the care and caress of the waves.

PART V

HOMECOMING
Mactan, Cebu, Philippines

The current seat of Catholicism in the country,
five centuries after Datu Lapu-Lapu of Mactan killed
the Portuguese conquistador Ferdinand Magellan

—January 13–15, 2023

Dispatches from Recovery

2024

So many ways to overwhelm a healing brain and yet so many ways to let it wither and atrophy. A dance we three are learning.

A grocery store is too bright and the never-ending shelves of shapes feel like they will topple and crash on my head. A restaurant is too loud, too many competing voices and too many utensils clanging. A party, a cinema, a gymnasium—places the woman I used to be frequented now make me feel overloaded, inundated, drowning, withdrawn.

Meanwhile, the quiet of the house can also be too much: too dulling, too diminishing, too lonely. "Use it or lose it," a neuro physical therapist said. Cocooned, my brain can't grow back what it lost: all that the blood was hungry for.

So Stephen and some friends found a way.

A pottery studio has just enough light and only the ambient sounds of water trickling, a wheel spinning, a kiln's heat rising and crackling against clay. At the pottery studio I can use my hands and will them to move. I can use them to scoop water from a bucket, to push and guide wet dirt. I can ask a classmate to please hand me more clay and the teacher to give me more directions, and I can repeat her instructions softly to myself to try to remember them.

At the pottery studio, I can focus on a task and make something on my own, of my own—but I am not alone. Side by side with people, it's the best place to be.

Talking to people, especially face-to-face, can be intimidating, confounding. But at the pottery studio, I can be shoulder to shoulder with someone, feel accompanied, and yet never have to meet the intensity of their stare, the demand for attention. At the pottery studio I practice speaking with my voice, listening with my ears, creating with my hands.

My left hand is still weak, so the vases and dishes come out wonky. The woman I used to be would find use for them, resourceful and creative as she was. The woman I now am finds humor in the lopsided ceramics. I hear her giggle, jokingly brag to the person next to her that the cup with the floppy lip is a signature piece, an imperfection no one can copy.

At the pottery studio, who I was and who I am sit at the wheel side by side, mixing dirt and water, dirt and water. Her turn. Then hers. Layering in was, is, and will be. Together.

23

Nostalgia Tour

Then there's the addicting nostalgia.

It's as if I've left the dark of the cinema and stepped into the screen before me, into the feature-length music video I've been replaying in my mind since 2003. When I've been unable to sleep these twenty years, this is where I sometimes go. To heartbreaking R&B, to girl-group pop, to percussion sounds from a parade, to the cracks in the voice of a local boy with the perfect swoop of hair that swished, if audibly, when he led me through a crowd of festivalgoers. These are the sounds of my teenage years, or at least a long weekend from then, the cream filling between the harder shells of a childhood that wouldn't stop emptying and a young adulthood that would always be at full capacity. When I can't sleep, I roll on my pillow, crane my neck, and bring my ear close to memories of this place where, for three days, my father and I had fun.

He had collected me from my sister, who had collected me, indefinitely, from my mother. He had business down south in Cebu, and it was Sinulog season, the best season there ever was. Hiding behind painted masks, everyone could be who they truly were, and so for a short but significant time, I learned of my papa's secret ability to put on something other than the costume of work or the worth he had tied to it. We danced. Not with each other, but around. I think unlike most fathers, he was relieved to see a boy take interest in me, a proxy or stand-in, so to speak. I was an old fifteen, a good kid. It was my father who was the delinquent, and I was the one acting like his keeper. With the swoopy-haired kid pulling me by my elbow, Papa could be free.

That's how I remember that weekend: not one of us with a care, moving to the same polyphonic sound of a city thrice-colonized. I could hear it then as I hear it now. The Chinese gong, the Spanish trumpet, the bright reprise like that of the end of an American ad, all carried by what's left of the Cebu, or Sugbu, Rajahnate: the higher octaves of temple sounds. Anouk's dancing to it now, and Stephen too, like I was and couldn't help it then. The song plays all day, all night, indoors and out. For a week, Kenny G. ceases to play in elevators and hotel lobbies, replaced by the happy, twinkly, percussive Sinulog song. Like it served as a buffer for me and my father two decades ago, it's now cushioning Anouk from the history lesson given to us at this morning's city tour, the history she won't accept and can't reconcile and refuses to smile at the camera for.

"But if they colonized these people, why are they praying and dancing to their god?" she said to me but loud enough for the tour guide to lose his place in the script.

We lagged behind. I tucked a hair behind her ear. Hushed, I said, "It's like, they took our baby gods and reimagined them, or we took their god and dressed him like the babies we worshipped and adored."

Sinulog is the festival, or, more accurately, the ritual prayer-dance, celebrating the brown-skinned baby Jesus in Spanish royal garb, an appropriation if there ever was one. In 1521, Ferdinand Magellan gifted would-be local allies, Rajah Humabon and his queen, with a Santo Niño, or an icon of the baby Jesus. It was a war tactic, a Trojan horse with a diaper on. The Rajahnate prayed to manitos, or little gods, and the conquistadors knew this. They used the intel to fashion an image out of another image, a trap. Who in a child-obsessed culture wouldn't welcome a baby? They embraced him, then embraced what he brought with him.

"I still don't understand, Ma," Anouk said, visibly perturbed, biting her nails. She dug her heel in the preserved wood of the historic house we were visiting. "Can we go home? I mean, to the hotel? My hip hurts."

Did it? Or did she want out?

I sure did. I told her we'd eat lunch early, cut to the part where we feast on lechon and puto bumbong and sip a sweaty glass of pandan shake. The tour guide didn't mind. He was a slow walker, even slower on stairs. We told him he was great and it had been so educational, but her hip disability was bothering her. We tipped him; he bowed to us. He whistled as he walked away from us and out the hotel lobby, glad to not have to drag us through many flights of temple, church, and shopping center stairs. Half the work, paid in full, and finally without a blunt American preteen questioning his rehearsed lines. She makes me proud. *On vacation, it's the little things.*

Now here we are at said lobby, uncontrollably clapping our hands, bobbing our heads, and swinging our hips to the Sinulog song performed by a local school band. For twenty minutes now, it's this catchy tune drowning out the sultry rhythms and blues playing from a rock-shaped speaker in the lobby fountain and the K-pop a gaggle of girls are choreographing to for their TikTok. I've stepped into the music video of my teens, I tell you. But twenty and a half years ago, I wouldn't have known to entrust my opinion or intuition with a parent just like that, like Anouk did. I remember the boy asking if I wanted to sneak away to the courtyard for face and body paint and maybe to make out, him asking another time because I hadn't responded. I was eavesdropping. Papa sat in a circle of friends and relatives, once again speechifying and holding an audience captive. He told them about a new venture and needing investors. And in that moment, a vision from the future came to me: us on separate planes, his crashing.

Papa and I, we did not have a language. We did not have the reciprocity that Anouk and I have. I knew that had I said anything, he wouldn't have understood. I kept my vision to myself and pulled the boy to the courtyard. Dolphins were all the rage in the aughts. I asked to be painted to look like a neon bottlenose juggling a soccer ball, which the boy, quirky as me and as well a footballer, liked. He kissed me, not even a little awkwardly. So I kissed him back. When he tried to kiss me again, I said one of two Cebuano phrases I knew: Dili na. It prompted him to speak Cebuano to me the rest of the night, which meant he was now just background noise to me, static to drown out the new knowledge of my father's second fall, the second big trough in his narrative arc, the cause for his relinquishing of me to a new parent, a new country. We all sometimes need distractions like that.

"How's your hip?" I ask Anouk.

She doesn't hear me. She's wide-eyed at the band, about to take their picture. When she squats down for a better angle, I know her hip is better—or that earlier it wasn't hurting at all. I just have a feeling she's nearly out of film. I search my purse for the Instax pack. When she presses down on the shutter button, nothing comes out, and when she turns around, my hand is already held out. She asks, "How'd you know, Mom?"

I could wink, but I'm not a winker. So I say, "Because, Bitty, I'm like you."

She knows what I mean: I step in and out of the past; I see the future.

Dispatches from Recovery

2024

It is springtime. Outside, the perennials and annuals I planted last year sprout unapologetically, as though they're to put the queen's gardeners to shame. Before the April air cools for the evening, I hope to gather a few blooms, gather them like Anouk's knowing of me, and stick the flowers in crystal I've repurposed from my mother-in-law's cupboard of special-days-only wares. I can step out onto the porch now and gather these flowers myself, having transitioned from a wheelchair to a walker to a cane.

"Can you believe you grew these?" Stephen asked me once at the hospital. Back then, I didn't believe or didn't want to believe. But belief, if we're honest, comes and goes—especially belief in oneself. And it turns out, I'm one for believing in tomorrow—as only a person is wont to do when they are daring enough to take The Gardener's Almanac *for gospel.*

24

Informal Settlers

We look like we rolled out of bed because that is exactly what we did. For there is nothing remarkable about today, nothing outside of how normal it all feels, that is exactly what we did. We are toward the end of our trip, that time when it feels more ordinary to be away than to be back home. It's that point in traveling when it's the specifics of your own house and your way within it, the look of it, the smell of it, that you're trying to recall. And so, this morning we climbed out from under the sheets. We slipped into swimsuits we had hand-washed the night before. We ate a fast but big breakfast. After we paid someone with a car to take us to someone with a boat, we paid that second someone to take us out to sea, to a triangle of islands and reefs in Cebu Strait. The transactions were just shy of being clandestine, and they scared us just enough to make us feel a kind of thrill and to ultimately be proud of our know-how at the end. Everyone's still got ten fingers, ten toes, is the way I see it. And maybe we got lucky. But that is exactly what we did. And this is exactly who I am now.

We ate another lunch on a boat—boat lunches are commonplace for us three now—and the fisherman we hailed out at sea and who paddled with his catch of urchin and bony fish is still on our boat with his net and mini gas grill. Anouk and I ate the seafood, and Stephen shared the grilled pork and rice the boater had packed, and we ate it all with our hands, flavoring our meals to each of our liking with the same bowl of chile vinegar, and when we were done, when we'd licked our fingers, we rinsed our hands in the ocean. To wash it all down, we had beer and coconut water purchased from another passing boat, and before we knew it, there were, are, seven of us on the rental when we had started out with four. It's been said: We are people who make friends on vacation.

The sea beyond is inky, the water slapping the sides of our bangka is a clear and minty blue. I'm full and I'm warm and the truest statement I can make, the best sentence I can possibly write today is: I am happy.

We anchored here momentarily in Nalusuan Marine Sanctuary so we could jump in and see more fish, then have our lunch. Stephen says to Anouk that he always wanted to snorkel when he was a boy, but nobody really took him because his parents were always tired, always wary of what's out there.

And she says, "And now you get to do it with me!" She smooshes his face between her hands.

They do their new secret handshake: bumping fists, then hands swimming through air, like a koi fish dance, like minnows chasing each other in the water.

At the last snorkeling stop, she and I had our own version of this reciprocity. Anouk swore she saw Marlin, and I swore I saw Nemo. Last night we learned that most clownfish sold in the United States are caught in the Philippines, the demand created by the popular film leading to a rapid decline of wild fish stock in our waters. We kept our sightings secret from the fisherman, albeit he fished for food and not aquaria, the principle behind it being that we weren't snitches, not ever to betray creatures of these reefs.

I look ahead to where Anouk sits, and she's singing a Blackpink song softly to herself and has one leg, her bad leg, pulled up to her chest—a habit from pain management, a signal to me to remind her to take care. I look back, and Stephen's treading water as the fisherman tinkers with his net, the two of them talking in Tagalog, those not-so-long-ago language lessons paying off. But I hear Stephen confuse *walo* (eight) for *wala* (none), and I hold up eight fingers to let him know. As he corrects himself, as he repeats what he just said a little slower and surer, his fingers go wild in the air, and I want to tell him that it means so much to me that he's made the loving effort and that he's made such homophones and false cognates and silly mistakes a part of our language.

He and the fisherman keep talking: how they fare in storms, how we made our way here. What life is like in a low-income sitio of Cebu, how isolated I can feel in South Carolina, how they each came to learn Tagalog. The fisherman comes to the end of the net string he's been untangling, and when he sees another boat of people looking hungry for lunch, he says the quickest of goodbyes, and he trips on his net and his words, assuring us of our delightful, fated meeting. "Twenty years!" he says, stretching a leg over to his boat. "Wag ganun katagal ulit! Okay? Okay?"

I wave and nod, agreeing to not wait another two decades before our next visit.

He starts his motor; our boater starts ours. We head to our last stop, to white sand Caohagan. We ride for twenty minutes, my hair already dry by the time we slow down for our approach. Long before the dock, we see that it's a residential island of shelters made of plywood and corrugated tin, like a satellite city floating on the water as that of the cruise ship in Jamaica.

The boater says, "Informal settlers."

Anouk asks what the phrase means.

I tell her that it's likely they can't afford to live on the mainland because of the country's long-standing and engineered poverty, because of the political corruption taking money away from public works and services, the very bequeathals from colonialism, so they've made a settlement of scrap wood and scrap metal houses here.

"And they're allowed?"

"Here, for now, yes. As long as the island isn't sold by the government."

This she understands. Her chest rises as she takes in air and information. "Granddad said it's okay I'm missing school because I'll probably learn more here." Sometimes my father-in-law surprises me, like there's a kindly, sophic sage hiding under the American masquerade of geocentricity and dominance, a truer self needing a coaxing out by some humbling journey. Anouk continues, "I'm learning so much about you and me and everyone, Ma."

She grabs her snorkel and slips on her flip-flops. I retie my swim dress. Stephen rebraids her hair and pulls lint off his unshaven chin. We straighten up wherever and however we can . . . out of reverence, out of kinship, out of the understanding that all of us here, and wherever else our often-forced itinerancy has taken us, are simply trying to make a home wherever and however we can.

Dispatches from Recovery

2024

My birthday is this weekend, and I cry about it four or five times a day, every time I remember that I almost didn't have another birthday, almost died at only thirty-seven. I tell this to my new therapist, someone I came to trust in no time at all and into whose practice I graduated when it was deemed less necessary for me to be in grief therapy and more beneficial to seek a life-change specialist (but perhaps they're one and the same?). Either way, I'm happy to no longer be in Tracy's flippant "care" and to instead have weekly appointments with Dr. Fields. This is our fourth session, and it's been wildly fortuitous to have been paired by my case manager with a professional whose mother also had a brain bleed and spent time fighting for her life and for her living on the same beige-and-white neuro unit as me. Whatever I say, whatever I bring to this new therapist, she genuinely understands.

She says, "You're crying because not only are you grateful, you're also suspended between belief and disbelief over what happened and how you've overcome. If being in these in-between places doesn't make us cry, I don't know what will. And if being in these in-between places doesn't make us grow, then Lordhavemercy."

I think about the two seconds that are either too soon or too late, and I hold them right there in my purview, just to the left of Dr. Fields and not too far from my belief and disbelief. I feel how close they are and how close we are, me and these contradicting truths. At the moment I also feel the weightlessness of hair regrowing where chemicals have made my scalp shed, and I feel the warmth of cinnamon squirming in my belly, the lush and spicy chai I proudly made on the stove all on my own today (nowadays, it's these little things that instill dignity). And I feel every move my body makes—the legs I cross tighter when I'm attentive and the way I lick my teeth when I'm thinking—because these movements are, after all, mine. Recently, there have been more mornings when I wake up feeling grateful to be here, to have time, to mark my passage in it, which is, come to think of it, the essence of memoir. I survived a brain aneurysm rupture, something that within a day kills half the people who experience it. I live to tell the tale. And I live to find a new way to tell it.

Dr. Fields likes the color yellow like my previous and, to put it nicely, second-rate therapist. In fact, today Dr. Fields is covered in a yellow beaming through our Zoom, and it's a yellow I don't hate, and it isn't a brightness that hurts my eyes or feels untrue. I accept it, like I've accepted the pair of delayed or advanced seconds that I know will follow me if not forever, for most of what is left of my time on this planet, in this universe. This too has felt less like an assault: My time here isn't one big setup bound to make me fail against expectations the woman I used to be must've built around herself to protect herself, a wall of expectations that was crumbling and pelting her for so long, too long, a time.

"What else is making you cry these days?" Dr. Fields asks.

I say, "That I don't know if I'll ever finish the book."

"Why wouldn't you?" she says, leaning into the screen.

My head falls back gently to meet the chair's pilled upholstery, snagged threads wispy against the skin just below my rupture site, reminding me of what is there and what isn't, like the small, faint shadow my cat is alert to and is chasing after along the wall. After a moment, I respond to Dr. Fields and say, my voice lower, "Because I don't have the same brain as the woman who set out to write it."

And as soon as the words leave my lips, I feel them fall beneath the surface of my terror to run with the current of my past life and past self, which are now both mostly hidden behind this midlife, post-traumatic coming-of-age but is still a current so very much coursing through me. An electricity that could, if I let it, charge me forth.

"That's hard," Dr. Fields says, "and that's a good thing. You'll layer her words and ideas with yours. And remember where your work and worth come from, what we talked about last time? How you might approach this big unknown?"

I know she's on to something because of late I've found myself struck by the breadth of things I don't yet know—the breadth of an open space, which is the primest place for a writer, because what is our work if not the work of exploration? And I really do love to write. Writing has sustained me since I was seven. It guarded me as an adolescent, shaped me into an adult, informed and grounded my motherhood, brought me closer to my two, to my closest friends, and time and again—including now, when I have limitations and needs stemming from a condition that could have killed me—to myself. I will write, and I'm already writing. Jane Austen wrote, "I was in the middle before I knew that I had begun."

"Yes, yes," I say, and inhale and pause. I take a moment to feel the combined energies of all the people, all of them survivors, I've ever been, and the combined force of all the questions I have yet to ask and pursuits I have yet to embark on.

When I continue, Dr. Fields continues with me, and I feel supported and assured, which, I've learned, is the only way forward in time and back into it. The only way home. It's not that this story ends nicely, and I get to write it without challenge. The comforting, steadying truth here is that while my new life and self are cognitive disabilities and physiological deficits galore, I'm not alone, never have been, and by the looks of it, might never be. So I say with Dr. Fields, as she looks at me with a gentle smile and I allow my gaze to land softly on the manuscript waiting patiently on the kitchen island, "My brain and life have changed, but my heart, from which my work and worth come, remains the same."

25

I Gave Her My World. I Gave It First to Me.

I can't give her what I don't have, is what I keep telling myself. They told me to give her the world. So I gave her *my* world, but before that, I gave my world back to me, which of course I couldn't do in just one visit. It all felt like an unbelievable forever, like ten days in the Philippines was both a way to return time, to stretch it and massage it, and to stop it. I'm back in a plane seat, strapped in as though against my will, with two masks on my face: one to cover my breathing and the other to conceal my crying. It is the most appropriate time to be at my most ridiculous. I'm sitting here, clasping a metal buckle on my lap again, considering if I should make a run for it.

We've been up for eighteen hours, without so much as a blink to interrupt or take away from our last hours here. I could call the day a blur, but it wasn't. The day was vivid to the teeth. Fast like a pickpocket's hands, spectacular and precise like it too. It was brisk, full, brimming in a way that made me feel like I am a tiny part of a ceaseless surge of humans in movement toward and yet away. Our carry-ons of hope, however illusory, powering us just enough so we can make something—ourselves—happen again.

This morning, eighteen hours ago, Anouk woke up with the kind of hip pain that comes when she's most anxious, as in before a standardized test or when she first heard the words *pandemic* and *lockdown*. As in when she's about to leave the place that made her mother sweet, quirky, resourceful, fun-loving, food-obsessed, and concerned with appearances just enough so she has, at least at the top of each semester, a new outfit to wow her school friends. Her hips developed uneven in utero, the right hitched up, pulling with it a buttock, a femur, a shin, and a heel that would always feel restless only to eventually lose sensation and then movement from overuse or underuse or sudden spikes or dips in emotion. Psychological factors stimulate inflammation, thus stiffening her hips, often to the point of disabling her.

Today was supposed to be Sinulog day. After island-hopping yesterday, we spent all afternoon and evening at the mall connected to our hotel by a skybridge. We scoured all six wings and all four floors of SM City Cebu for festival wear, using our dwindling stash of pesos on a rainbow of feathers, gold headbands, blue and purple beads, and cotton tees to rip up and have braided and embellished by artisans at a craft kiosk. She'd prepared everything: our orthopedic shoes ready by the hotel room door; the headdresses atop our crafty, floral outfits; and the pea-sized toothpaste already on the bristles of our toothbrushes so all we needed was to wet them for use in the morning. But the pain, I knew what kind it was right away. She woke up looking stunned, and when she wakes up like that, I remember why they call it a "stun gun."

If we were home, I would have microwaved a wet washcloth already and would have prepared an ice pack for after the warm compress. As I prepare the first parts of the RICE regimen, Stephen would be gathering and moving things around to create a place in front of the television for compression and elevation. One of us would be sending her teacher a note. But today, our variables were a towel soaked in hot tap water, ice in a hotel laundry bag, and down pillows stacked on one side of the hotel bed. "A little rest," I told her, then small exercises the physical therapist had taught us. I didn't want to lie, so when she asked if we could still make the parade, I said, "You know, Bits, there's a kind of parade at the mall too."

When she could move, I helped her into her festival clothes. We took photos. She forced a smile. She remembered the yellow fan she'd bought as an accessory, with the painted-on flowers that matched her headdress, and asked if I could find it in her bag. "I'm ready," she said, and I knew she meant she was ready for breakfast, for the day, for the adjustments we needed to make, for whatever those final hours here could still, and will, offer us.

She fanned herself in the elevator made of mirrors, amused by this show and coming-together of her Filipinoness. Long brown-black hair, beaded accessories, a temporary tattoo still unfaded from our rainy day on Cowrie Island, a Spanish fan that her grandmother—my mother—would have kept in her purse, and a whirl of memories from my own colorful youth, plus a pocketful of cash converted from American dollars she'd been saving from her Lunar New Year envelopes. If she's not a historical artifact, I don't know what is.

I held her up by hooking my arm under her armpit, and that was enough support to give her the balance she needed to watch her head tilt this way and that in the mirror, as girls her age do. *That's it,* I remember thinking, *that's what I have to do to get her through this day, through the pain.* Amusements. Sensorium. We'll ride Sinulog fever into delirium and coax the festive spirit even when we're missing the parade.

At breakfast, we ate everything, as always. We watched the parade from my phone, which rested against my coffee cup. YouTube acted as a teleporter. It returned time, sped it up, divided it, allowing my girl to be at two places at once while partially immobilized. By the sixth school band and dance group, we'd had our fill. The dancers' costumes were still distinct, but the choreography began to repeat. A relief, to not have woken up early and made the four-mile trek to a muddy stadium with a limping child on my or Stephen's back.

I gave her leg another stretch. Stephen told her we could go as slow and make stops as necessary, to which she responded with a pivot on the good heel, so through the lobby crowd we went and there was no turning back now.

Arriving at the mall entrance was like arriving at the most flamboyant Cirque du Soleil tent. Mothers, fathers, grandmothers with walkers, and children carted around in various contraptions with wheels. Teenage girlfriends were there too. Somc brought along suitors. Everyone had come to the mall in festival wear—some families in matching screen-prints, others in the same shade of do-it-yourself henna or the same beige raffia skirt. It cost to go to the parade, or at least to culminate your pilgrimage, your ritual prayer-dance, at the newly built stadium the new mayor had been bragging about. I don't know why I was surprised to see a mass of Cebuanos and visitors celebrating instead at the comfortable, no-entry-fee, air-conditioned mall.

"Ma! Mom! Look!" Her famous words returned. She limped toward the mall atrium, the shaft of vertical space cutting through the middle of every floor. When she found a part in the crowd, she wiggled her body in and held a hand back, fully expecting that I'd be there to be pulled with her toward the glass from where we'd watch the dancers below. Stephen stood behind the crowd. He was the tallest person wherever we went, and so a nosebleed seat still gave him a mosh-pit experience.

Performing in that moment was a group from an island smaller than Mactan, whose costumes drew inspiration from farther back in time. Precolonial. Foot-tall feathers fanned out from their hairlines and wrapped around their necks like rooster collars. The women wore beaded leather high-cuts; the men wore short, fringed kilts made of hide in a deeper brown. Beyond that, tattoos everywhere. Water signs. Arrowheads. Cockfighting spurs. Eight rays of the sun, symbols for the eight provinces first to revolt against Spain. I was a sympathizer, ready to be inked right there. Now this was a Sinulog she and I could fully get behind.

More rounds of dancers came through the stage. We stayed for a number of them until crouching down crimped her hip to the point of it needing another stretch. I hooked my arm around her again, setting her weight off her right leg. We found a seat. We rested. We took our time. We stretched. Then we were off again to be surprised, over and over, by a group of dancers and their percussionists and saxophonist and trumpeter arousing a crowd outside a Uniqlo, an Ace Hardware, a dried mango kiosk, a Baltic sea salt soap stand where they kept handing me samples and I kept taking them. (I'll take anything if it's free.)

Every performance lasted an entire song, sometimes with an encore too, and that was about all the time Anouk had before she needed to sit again or be lifted by one of us. Several repeats of this, and I was breathless from both the marvelous performances and the task of being her human crutch. Oh, but I loved being that crutch, the lean-on. I felt like a happy appendage, an extension of circuitry connected to the excitement flowing through her. What else would I offer? Here's the sensory she needed, the distraction I planned. We hoped for an overload, and I was conferee to all that now. *Pile us up,* is what Stephen and I kept saying with our bodies and our voices. I might have even actually whistled at something once. I believe Stephen attempted a PG-13 modification to a twerk.

Alas, it was time for lunch. We *excuse-us*'d our way to the escalator. Descending to the food court, I was taken back to my childhood once more. All it took was one whiff of frying oil and fried potatoes, and I knew: Potato Corner was within my reality. My favorite childhood snack, which my brother stole and sold car parts for, was french fries shaken in a tub of sour cream and barbecue-flavored powder. If there was anything good that came out of American occupation, it was french fries, and my brother and I became juvenile delinquents for them. To honor the spirit of delinquency, I dashed down the escalator and weaved through people, who became annoyed. “Ano ba yan!” they said.

I held my hand up like a bicycle flag, in hopes that Stephen and Anouk could trace my path to the potatoes. They eventually found me. I was in line for something worth all my money, which at that point, really wasn’t much. She needed to sit again, but my french fries! Stephen waited in line for twenty minutes and bought me the biggest, aptly called *tera*, which was one up from *giga*, and I could have kissed him on the mouth right there, but instead I sent him off again, to the kimbap and biko stands, because I had one goal today and that was to receive so I could give.

When I popped a fry in my mouth, all the artificial flavor just about betrayed every health kick I’ve ever allowed myself as an adult, thank heavens, and it was the taste of my brother’s love and of our collective strength. Garlic powder. Onion powder. Fructose. Green flecks supposed to look like scallion pieces. We were just kids. What were we stealing for? We knew how to make a profit, that’s the truth, however one looks at it. At the end of the day, my brother, my kuya, and I, we bought ourselves fake potatoes in fake flavorings, and we felt like we’d won the most authentic dish of any cuisine. *That’s what matters,* the look of pleasure on my face says to Anouk. Fried potatoes, mashed potatoes, au gratin. What matters is that you liked it, is that it gave you new, or at least familiar, language for what it’s like to be you on this planet, in this universe, in this lifetime. It’s also what matters about claiming home or ancestry, or writing books, for that matter: It gave you, you.

When she tried it for the first time, those first few bites produced just one true reaction: “Ma, no wonder your brother stole for you! It’s so good; slay, Mama!” She’s her trendy tween self again, Gen-Alpha-ing her way through lunch with hand signs she’s thankfully explained to me.

After our meal, it was just right to keep giving in to my nostalgia. I remembered a makeup shop from my teen years, and we went there.

I had about 5,000 pesos left, the equivalent of ninety or so dollars, and spent 400 of it on a shade of cheek tint I'd been looking for, for twenty years. The makeup, too, was a part of giving back to myself.

We visited the costume exhibit at the farthest wing of the mall, where the local university had displayed a Met Gala–worthy curation of ornate dresses with skirts as wide as a table and golden headdresses as tall as a wedding cake. Each was donated by a former Sinulog festival queen, and they amused Anouk like I'd hoped. That really isn't strong enough: The dresses baptized her with a familiar desire.

"Oh my gosh, oh my gosh! I wanna go to fashion school like you," she said.

"Babe, I dropped out of fashion school." I wanted to make it clear. "But Auntie Buki and Aunt Nancy finished."

"Yeah, but you still make our Halloween costumes . . . and things for our house." She wasn't wrong. "You started. I'll finish."

After the exhibit, I wanted to shop for pasalubong for friends and family: gift bags of dried mango, gift boxes of flaky otap, sachets of made-here shampoo meant to keep our black hair black. By the time we're done, I can see Anouk's adrenaline waning. "One last stop," I told them.

"I don't want to leave," she said.

I told her we could come back to the mall after a quick rest at the hotel.

"No. I don't want to. I don't want to leave here!" she yelled. She's not once raised her voice or shown attitude on this trip. She rarely ever does.

I pulled her to me. I searched my lexicon, my body, for something equally kind and true. "The pets are waiting for us, Bits. They miss us."

She mumbled into my chest, and I had to rely on our language to understand what she was saying. "Yeah, you're right, Bits. Everyone here *is* so kind."

She peeled her face from my dress. "And happy."

I echoed whatever she said. "And happy."

"And helpful."

"And helpful."

"And generous."

"And generous."

"And loving."

"And loving, so loving."

I was a better person already. Nothing she said was false, and yet none of it negated the hard truth of what, and who, I'd survived as a child. My heart was expanding right there, or maybe it was feeling how much it had expanded in the previous ten days. Nakakataba ng puso. A big heart has room for conflicting interests, for multiple realities. A place that once hurt me can also love me. And I can say the same about America: A place that rewards me can, and does, take away from me.

We kept standing there, teary, blocking foot traffic, Stephen to the side of us with our shopping bags and looking sorry and staring at his feet. When I landed an essay in a big online magazine, Stephen brought home a tiramisu from Whole Foods, which had been, and remains as, our favorite celebratory treat. He'd read the essay but thought we'd read it again, together, while sharing our dessert. When we scrolled to the end, we saw the only comment: "Go back to where you came from, you useless parasite!"

It was an essay about being an immigrant mom wary of driving and travel and a meditation on how my bicycle and Anouk's bike trailer allowed us to move through our neighborhood, and life, in tandem. I thought of that online troll and their comment as we three stood there in the mall corridor, weighed down by bags of dried mango and the grief that's already settled before we'd even stepped foot on the plane. I thought of the comment and for the rest of the afternoon entertained the fantasy: go back to where I came from. Not seriously, I don't think, but it turned out Anouk was fantasizing the same.

"We could just live here. You can write from anywhere."

"But Dad's job?"

"If he really wants to go back to his job, he can send us money!"

Even I was shocked, and shaken, by her proposition. "Bitty. You don't mean that. We're a team, remember? You said that. We could never live away from Dad."

A push, a pull. Isn't that the immigrant story they want?

"Then I don't know, Mom. You're so happy here. And Dad's happy when you're happy."

I tried to search my lexicon and my body again for something kind and true. I pulled her to me once more. And Stephen pulled us to him, and I could smell the sweet smell of mangoes in the shopping bags in his hands and the smell of freshly laundered linens, which is what he'd always smelled like even when we were in our twenties, and it's the clean smell that's always comforted me. When I travel for work, I bring a T-shirt of Stephen's to lay on the hotel pillow, and just like that, as corny as it is and as much as literary critics would hate me for saying it, it brings me home. I am a Filipina writing a Filipino American story. It's all bound to have a cheesy romantic twist, is it not? There's no way it can't end up against a tragic-comic backdrop.

We caught our breaths and gathered ourselves. After all that, I could only make one suggestion: spend our last pesos on clothes for the plane. This, too, was part of our language. Anouk immediately perked up. It was post-Christmas, so the retailers were a bit barren, but still we found our travel outfits. When Anouk pulled a very Y2K smiley-print pullover from the racks, I felt time twist into itself again, warping as colorful sand art does. It's what she's wearing now in the plane seat next to me, and she's looking more and more like my teen self with every passing moment, with every start and end to an in-flight movie or meal. But then again, Buki said that it's me who looks like her. *Uncanny, uncanny, uncanny.*

When we'd been rung up, the hip pain had become a numbness that took feeling away from her leg. She couldn't walk, not even assisted. Stephen picked her up, leggy girl that she is. I walked behind them. Her legs dangled like they did when we'd walk-rock her back to sleep after she was woken up by night terrors that came frequently between hospitalizations in her preschool years. When she had night terrors, I worried that my bad memories had transferred to her cache somehow, that imprinted on her were rather terrible, horrific parts of me. The doctor assured us that night terrors were normal for that age, but only now am I accepting that I have something good to give. *Give her the world,* they said. So I gave her my world, which is a kind, happy, helpful, generous, loving, so loving, world. It's the world I gave back to me.

A sign welcomed us at the hotel. The pool, which had been undergoing remodeling, had reopened suddenly, if not miraculously. PLEASE ENJOY, the sign said.

"They opened it just for me, Ma," Anouk said.

"Of course they did," I assured her.

I'd already washed, line-dried, and packed our swimsuits, but it didn't matter. It's what she needed. Water, or swimming in it, heals her.

She and Stephen played in the pool, and I watched them from the hotel room window as I packed some more. We're more extravagant with ourselves now, but we're still cheap and don't want to pay for check-in. I rolled mango packets inside shirts and shampoo packets inside shoes, and the more fragile items, like flaky otap and mother-of-pearl coasters I'd bought for our house, went in the carry-on compartment for my nowhere-to-be-found laptop. I let my two stay in the water until it was six hours before our plane's departure to leave us time for showers, a last food-court dinner, a hip flexor stretch, the checkout process, and the traffic that was sure to meet us through the city on a festival night.

We capped our evening, our long-awaited vacation, with fried chicken, another tera-sized Potato Corner, rice cakes, and glass noodles. *Why, yes, one of everything, please.*

Anouk and I cried again. Stephen fetched us more paper napkins to cry into. It was just past nine o'clock, a little less than four hours before our plane's departure. I began to worry about airport traffic and told them it was time to retrieve our bags from the hotel. But the mall kept filling with people, like a last call for the bar at a wedding. I stammered, giving instructions to my two. There wasn't much to bus, but I take up a high-handed attitude when I'm nervous. I was patting around the table for more things for them to throw away or recycle or pack up when the announcement was made: Jericho Rosales, my childhood celebrity crush, will be singing on the food-court stage to officially close Sinulog season.

"Oh my gosh! Oh my gosh!" I kept yelling, sounding like Anouk. I stood on a chair to see him. He waved at the crowd. I swear he looked my way and said, "Maayong gabii, guapa!"

I started to cry harder and couldn't hold my phone steady for a decent photo or video. Stephen took the phone from me and captured me in my teenybopper moment. He looked at me through the phone screen, and I don't know what he sees when he sees me like that. But I'm me, again, a sixteen-year-old girl yet to be ripped from the only home she'd ever known.

Jericho sang a song my brother used to always play on our cassette player: "Forevermore" by Side A. I knew every line; every Philippine-born '90s kid does. I sang with Jericho and the crowd of hundreds. My voice cracked because I was sobbing. Anouk wiped tears from my face and held my hand, which was raised above my head, worship-service style. Amusement. Sensorium. Her mother belting out words she was pulling from deep within her memory. I turned around and sang her a line about spending all those goddamn years longing, dreaming, watching stars fall down, wishing something to be mine. That something: him, her, home. Myself.

It's been me all along.

I didn't want to leave, but I didn't want to be there when the song ended. I knew that after the bridge, the song wraps up after two rounds of the chorus. I hopped off the chair. "Let's go," I told them, and they were quite startled by my abrupt move.

When an editor friend, also Manila-born, took me out on one of those editor-writer brunches last fall, he asked why, unlike him, I still called the Philippines home. We'd both been away from it for two decades, had made lives and careers on the East Coast. I asked if he was asking as an editor, and he said he was asking as a friend.

I felt safe and said, "Because I was ripped from it, and there's an unfinished selvage to who I am."

I wanted to leave the song—and the moment—like that unfinished selvage, like the raw feeling you get when you've woken up from an unresolved dream, or the unease a baby being burped might feel, or the frustration from when the cable or power goes out in the last minutes of a televised game. Like the irresolute title and point of the song: forevermore.

Before I switch my phone to Airplane Mode, I find the song on iTunes and download it. I have it ready for takeoff, earbuds connected to my phone as opposed to the plane-seat screen. We lift off. I press Play simultaneously on iTunes and on the interface of Korea Air's free entertainment. I listen to the unfinished song, which was like the never-ending collective hum, and I hum to it as the scary movie plays before me, making it the soundtrack to a film no longer terrifying to me.

Anouk pulls my right earbud off so I can hear her. "Mom," she says. "Can we come back?"

Give her the world, they kept telling me. So I gave her my world. So I gave it first to me.

I search my lexicon, and my body, for something kind and true, and there are no appropriate words, just gesture. I give her my hand to shake, as a promise. She gives me hers, as collateral. Outside the plane window the city lights blur, and Stephen watches them. He's lost again, enraptured, and I like to think he sees me in all the stars and in all the festival fireworks shooting up to the sky and in the tangle of traffic below. I'm all those lights, and I'm not. I am there, and I am here too. I dip in and out of the past. I see the future. I tell stories in circles.

I look just like her.

She's completely herself, not an avatar of me.

I gave her my world. I gave it first to me.

She's falling asleep now. It's 2:00 a.m.

Jet lag will be a pain when we get back to our house on the quiet bend. But that's for tomorrow, which in Eastern Standard Time is today.

Today is tomorrow is until then. Yesterday will happen again.

Forevermore.

We'll come back. I made a promise.

Her eyes stop fluttering. She's deep in sleep.

I follow her cue. I stop the movie. I close my eyes.

The song goes on. I fall into a deep sleep, into a new time, into a new dream.

It's been me all along.

DISPATCHES FROM RECOVERY

2023

If I could have split time in two, I'd have parted it at the point just before my mind could, on command, generate more than one vision of a place that settled me. This is important. I'd been told that in times of distress, all I can control is where my mind goes. During those last, animal pushes, desperate to bring my daughter into the world, I heard the doula and midwife say this. During a panic attack, it was what I heard from my therapist through the phone. "Go to your happy place, Cinelle." What materialized on the screen of my mind both times—and countless more—were the lilies and ivy and koi pond and purple delphinium at the Central Park conservatory gardens. It's where Stephen and I proverbially and—because I'm the somewhat superstitious kind of Filipino—literally tied the knot. We were surrounded by forty-eight friends and family members. But by 2020, ten years since the happy day, I'd relied on the same memory so much that I could no longer protect the image of it from the protraction of the war of millennial life. Some work outsourcing or load redistribution had to happen. But so true and unfortunate was this: Before the pandemic, to say that my options were limited was to be generous. I had one happy place. But in the moments following a brain aneurysm rupture, as I lay on a stretcher, my head secured to it by a polyester band that pulled at my baby hairs while my cranium was filling with blood and my cerebellum drowning, a siren blaring above me and announcing the emergent moment, I was thinking of a particular hammock in Puerto Rico, a breezy rental in Jamaica, and a sandbar in the Philippines, and not only was I going to these happy places but feeling immense gratitude to and for myself that I had gone. That, of late, the sounds of these destinations had become the silent drumbeat of my days. If I died that night, I'd have that to claim. They would have that to say about me.

She'd traveled.

She'd finally gone home.

She gave her daughter the world—she gave it first to herself.

I know, and my loves know, where I now go when my eyes close.

EPILOGUE

I felt well enough to write (by hand) for fifteen to thirty minutes a day by spring 2024. With the help of volunteer typists such as my husband and my dear friend Jill, I finished the first draft of the *Travel + Leisure* essay I had begun writing when the aneurysm ruptured in my brain. Exactly a year since that life-changing day, my editor and I signed off on a final draft ready for printing the following February. I found it fitting to end *A Way Home* with the expanded version of this travel story, one that celebrates the strength that can only be found in community.

Let It Wash Over You

Travel + Leisure, The Water Issue, February 2025

Let me tell you about creative destruction. It might feel rude to call a catastrophe, like a hurricane or brain aneurysm rupture, "creative," but I'm interested here in its modifying the second of the terms, of "destruction," as if what we do with what has happened takes back the power snatched from us by the leveling winds or the cranial hemorrhage. Of course I'm not here to glorify "resilience." Not me, an immigrant and childhood trauma survivor fed up with empty platitudes like "What doesn't kill you makes you stronger." I'm here, instead, to remember what the Mississippians taught me at the end of my Act II: the period of recovery following a storm is the primest of times for strengthening a joyous, fruitful perspective, and for fashioning out of what remains not only a new reality but a closer truth.

I'd just flown back from the Mississippi Gulf, still blissful and grateful for the luck I found at every turn of the trip. I'd sat down, east-facing, at a café to write this very travel essay that I hope you're cautiously holding in your hands. I'd borrowed a charger from a man drinking an Americano. In return, I loaned him my pen. The barista had ensured it was oat milk frothing in my mug. It was, you might say, like any other day. But as I suppose is what happened when Katrina or Camille hit, life, as I knew it, was over in a matter of minutes. Something clapped in my head and before I could place my hand where I felt the thunder, the floor and walls were above me. Everything was in orbit: the charger, the pen, my coffee, and laptop. The sun burned my eyes and suddenly even the blue light of my phone and computer were unbearably bright. I tried to turn away, but my neck was locked in place. I closed my eyes. Feeling around for my phone, muscle memory allowed me to text my husband an SOS. Four hours later, at the ER, he was told I'd had a brain aneurysm, and to gather himself and his things and our daughter, and follow the ambulance to a larger hospital's neurological ICU.

Today, months since, I've fought to regain strength, a sense of self, and my ability to write and any interest in doing so, and I live with short-term memory loss as a result of traumatic brain injury. I sit here now fluent in the languages of neuroscience and neuropsychology for reasons I wish were more academic and less out of medical necessity. And I am looking through photos from my trip and reading what I'd started to draft on that life-changing day, and many lines fail to make sense because they were being composed as my brain started to drown in blood, and many details I'd spewed onto the page then now elude me. But indelible, even after brain surgery, is the fact that coastal Mississippi taught me that to be creative is to hope. Coastal Mississippi was my last long-term memory. It would guide me in recovery.

Here's what I'll never forget:

When Michelle, my Lyft driver, pulled up outside the Gulfport-Biloxi airport, she greeted me like I was an old friend coming to her daughter's wedding. She insisted on loading my suitcases into her trunk. "Let me help you," she demanded, then joked, "What you got in here? A million dollars for the casino?"

I quipped back, "Yeah, if I win, I'll share with ya."

And again, like we'd shared a youth, she replied, "No, you won't." And we rode the whole forty minutes to my first stop in Bay St. Louis (pronounced "Lewis") back and forth and quick like that. Michelle had encyclopedic knowledge of what had been made and remade on the coast after each hurricane, most notably Katrina, showing me new boardwalks connecting glittering resorts and mom-and-pop shops, and narrating the sustained cycles of destruction and rebuilding. Everywhere I turned, whatever I saw, I only had massive envy for what was evident: creation, re-creation, and an obedience to this heart-first, full-throttle getting on with life. I started to believe right then that try as others might to reduce the place to a narrative of survivorship, it was defined not by what calamities it had had to overcome, but by the openness it maintains despite compounding reasons to shut in and self-preserve. June Jordan, a poet and child of immigrants, said something akin to this coastal Mississippi philosophy: "To begin is no more agony than opening your hand."

After Michelle dropped me off at the Pearl Hotel, it was a late lunch with Ken, the photographer assigned to this story, and a verbose ambassador from the tourism board. What I remember of that extended lunch is having forgotten that we were in a public place. If I didn't fact-check now, I'd be close to thinking we were on her porch, rocking the swing and drinking from sweaty heirloom crystal she'd have told us the provenance of.

What else I remember of that first day was the safety I'd felt as a solo traveling woman, petite at five foot three, although that may mean nothing, wandering around town at day's end, in search of late-night provisions and a souvenir shop less of the magnets-and-shot-glasses kind and more of the like offering something I could later cook, plant, or otherwise work with my hands.

The shops, most of them housed in restored historic edifices seemingly competing for Most Romantic, were closing when I arrived, brooms a-sweeping and rugs rolling up, and yet—and there was that openness again—"Come in, it's all right," the shopkeepers said.

I recall going to bed the good kind of tired—the kind that finally silenced whatever trace amount of travel anxiety I had because dinner at the chef's table at Thorny Oyster was luxurious but unpretentious and so there was no tossing in bed and mulling over something gauche I might have said like when I'm socially misplaced and trying to fit in. There was only the satisfaction from the six courses that began with seared tuna and ended with my new knowledge for how long the coastline was: sixty-two miles to be exact. I'd traverse the mileage, riding shotgun to Ken, in four felicitous days.

Morning came and with it the sound of hulls slicing through the sound, and as well hollers from wedding parties mussing up outfits, already late for their bridal party breakfast, and the call of a hungover wife to a hungover husband standing on the pier-side of the street with pastries and coffees in hand. Seabirds gawked, perched on artfully carved oaks catty-corner from my hotel room balcony. Nautical flags and banners for charity events flapped in the breeze in the near distance, and I was certain I'd hit upon an American coastal town if there ever was one, this one having the neighborly sweetness of Stars Hollow, the tease of Salem in mid-fall, and the colorways of nearby Louisiana State University.

It was November, and most homes hadn't yet taken down their Halloween decorations, which made sense once I sat down with Ashley Planchard of the Mockingbird Café for a chat over a house-recipe chai and cinnamon loaf. The café had become the town's public living room after Katrina, and Planchard told me she had an outrageous love for her home. Planchard attends the town's Dolly Should Festival (a tribute to Ms. Parton) and Frida (Kahlo) Fest, which the café also sponsors, and is an annual participant in the "Witches Walk," on the Saturday before Halloween. I sorely regretted having come a week too late and alone, without my own mini-witch, my tween daughter. But Ashley assured me next year's festival would be here before we knew it.

While she continued about the town's rituals, I multitasked (one of the last times my brain would be capable of the feat), frantically jotting notes while scheming already about a possible return with my girl. And that's when I knew that as early as then, I'd made a connection with the place, which is to say, its people. Isn't that what a worthwhile destination does? Remind you of a particular someone you'd like to come there with? A place not only you'd revolve back to but with someone you love, who coaxes the magical and innovative out of you, and whose worldview you're helping to shape? And the worldview in Bay St. Louis and, I'd learn soon, every which way on Highway 90, was clear: Destruction is sure to visit us in this life, no matter who or where we are, and the only way to fare is to have an open hand and borrow from our neighbors, say, from the west of them, from New Orleans, a Bontemps attitude, and from just northeast, an outlook formed by the state's natural and agricultural abundance. We ought to know what and who we have. Make with which and with whom a good life. Remake said life many times over together if we must.

Full of practical and philosophical food, and carbohydrates, it was fitting to go on another aimless walk, between the tracks and the sea, and since my girl was already on my mind, when a parade of bubbles danced past, I followed it to a donkey milk soap shop and thereafter a gift shop with a bright green exterior with an equally perky name: Fleurty Girl. But that's where I was mistaken: I was the attraction there, in the best way. The workers and owner flocked to me like they were seabirds and I was a beachgoer with a sandwich. They wanted to tell me about everything, but less in a salesy way and more in a manner I recognize in my own people, the Filipinos: We're proud of who we are, what we have, what we can share, even if it's just delight. When my gaze landed on a Dolly candle or Beyoncé shirt, they became shoulder to shoulder with me in a jiffy to announce whose hands poured or sewed what. My attention became a kind of accelerant. The more things my eyes or fingers landed on, the more they said and all the quicker. It was exhilarating to be in their company, that if I were at all a rock star I would've murdered a cigarette and written an anthem right there. And as sequined as the merchandise and the owner's outfit were, it all somehow still had a homespun sincerity to it: this store was a curation by someone with a rags-to-riches story, whose sprightly creativity and infectious entrepreneurial spirit (she also owns themed Airbnbs) root down deep into a joy meant to be the kind of justice we survivors give ourselves. I left that store fortified in spirit, and that feeling I later summoned back in the radiology room, on the operating table, when my spine cracked as I stood again for the first time.

Ken texted and asked where I wanted to go next, and I was high on Fleurty Girl energy, so I said we should venture out toward Biloxi and see not what we find but what finds us. When we arrived at a dockside eatery, shrimps and oysters frittering on hot plates around us, Ken needed to change camera lenses. He pointed-and-shot to test his aperture, his new lens zooming into a fleet of shrimp boats, to which he called my attention. I'd told him on our drive that I wanted to interview fellow Asian Southerners. And because my telling him was an act of asking for help, the Gulf once again rewarded my grace. I ran to the fleet, introduced myself as a travel writer, and hopped onto boats when I was invited to, which was every time. Then I met Kim Pham, a shrimp boat operator from Vietnam, who was pleased to learn I'd grown up in the Philippines. She'd been a refugee there in the 1970s. We talked about her exodus—Vietnam, Philippines, Atlanta, the Gulf. I took her as a person who, like me, if provided a chance to stay in their motherland and a life in which war hadn't fractured humans from humans and from their homes, would prefer these alternate realities. But, like me, she'd also made something out of what she'd been handed, and evolution remains our constant state. She'd worked at a factory in Biloxi until it moved operations to Mexico. Again, she had to pick something from her past and alchemize it into a new present.

She'd been shrimping for more than two decades and the past couple of years had been the slowest, she said. Imported stock was swallowing the market whole, but as fierce as the competition was, fiercer still was the look in her eyes when she told me that her kids were grown and she'd follow them wherever they go, learn a new skill in yet another new trade if she had to, again, reinvent. As I was stepping off their boat, she practiced the impossible Francophone syllables of my name and gave me a thumbs-up—and I'll never forget the gesture and in fact mimic it when I wake up post-surgery and my husband says the one word I needed hearing: *Cinelle*.

An afternoon on the docks was wearing me out, or perhaps the blood vessel that would soon rupture had begun to leak and cause incredible fatigue. I asked Ken if we could cover a location or activity on the mellow side. "Let's just drive around," he said, and I'm glad he did because when we spotted the sculptural metal exteriors of the Ohr-O'Keefe Museum of Art, itself looking like gallant sails, I understood suddenly the meaning of the word "flagship" in all its maritime, realty, and metaphoric uses. There we discovered coastal Mississippi's long art history, including through an exhibit of works by Southern Prize and State Fellows and the City of Biloxi Center for Ceramics. Inside the latter I would slink my way and make a new acquaintance with, it seemed, the sole local potter not attending the whopping ceramics festival Ken and I had decided to forgo due to my diminishing strength. Her name was Georgia Sparling and she, like many others during the pandemic, boomeranged home to a Mississippi life full of outdoorsy activities, like kayaking, and crafty hobbies, such as pottery. Inviting opportunity, I told her I was curious about the Pascagoula River, and like the women who'd anointed my steps from the airport, through Old Bay, and off the docks of Biloxi, Georgia was at the ready to not only share information but go as far as making calls to her kayaking group. By that evening, before I could even learn where the blow dryer lived in my new hotel room, she'd arranged an afternoon on the water with two boater brothers, kayaks, and a boat large enough for Ken to do photography parkour and me to sit back in but slender enough to maneuver the Pascagoula's arteries.

With them that next day, I learned to say *ba'ou* instead of *bye-you*, and that wood treated with brackish water will withstand a storm better than anything you can buy at Home Depot. Cans of beer were popped open and raised, and while one of the brothers suggested entertaining us with his bluegrass-y tenor, we all decided the song of pluff mud and Spanish moss swaying in the breeze was music enough.

I remember that we drove off at golden hour, Georgia and her kayaking group waving goodbye as the sun moved down and west, and I was tired again, but Ken and I had been chasing good light the entire trip to get the best possible photos we could capture. I wanted more shots of the water, birds, cypress and oak, family picnics—and while in my better judgment now, I know to not push myself and to honor the limits protecting me from worse health, I do and ever will prize every shot Ken has since shared with me. I've lost plenty: tolerance for sensorium, physical stamina, mental focus. I'll always have, on a digital cloud and in my hippocampus, episodic memory that turns off my fear mode almost automatically: a lifelong benefit of travel—and travel writing—I'm increasingly understanding as absolutely crucial to my recuperation and longevity. And this is where I hope to take this essay next: We ought to think of the Mississippi Gulf not as a forgotten coast but a secret one waiting to be pried open not just for the varieties of pleasures it can give us but for the characters that could people the narratives we write about ourselves, because it's these happenstance social connections that enable the reward circuits of our brains, especially when we're at our weakest. Everyday life is largely, though not exclusively, controlled by subconscious processes. We're creatures of habit—and more. My trip to Mississippi, the contours of which formed by the serendipitous interactions that filled the time, pulled me away from domestic and journalistic routine, focusing my cognitive resources on all things peripheral yet essential: my Lyft driver's jokes; the welcome ambassadors' gossip; the diva energy of Dolly, Beyoncé, Frida, and Fleurty Girl; craftsmanship; the kindness of strangers; new friendships that hearken back on old you. The doctors and nurses asked me the same question several times a day for weeks: *Can you tell us who you are?* My answer changed every time, none of it alarming the medical team save perhaps for a puzzling one. I'm a writer who makes friends on travels. I admit it was quirky, but I am quirky. I was relearning. After brain surgery, whatever you're able to recall becomes your new self. My grief therapist puts it this way: *You become what you have, not what you've lost.*

Days after waking up, my husband read me online and handwritten notes from all over, including ones from Bay St. Louis, Biloxi, and Ocean

Springs, which was my last stop. I stayed at Gulf Hills Hotel & Resort, a fifty-seven-room waterfront hotel that was originally built in 1927 and was being restored to its former glory, having been partially destroyed by Hurricane Camille in 1969 (and, after being rebuilt, destroyed a second time by a fire in 1974). It fell into neglect over the following decades, but reopened in the fall of 2023.

The new owners, including Roxy Condrey, worked meticulously to revive a property where Marilyn Monroe, Judy Garland, and Jayne Mansfield once swam, water-skied, and sundowned with cocktails in hand. As part of the restoration process, Condrey and the team reached out to former guests and asked what they remembered. Most replied not with architectural details, but interactions. There was a teen, now a retiree, who'd hung out with a young Elvis, who loved staying in Villa 9 in the early 1950s. It's stories like this that Condrey and the team used to reclaim what the property had.

At the nearby Bozo's Too, I met up with my dear friend Rénard's family for lunch. Although he now lives in Charleston, he'd arranged for me to meet up with his mother, sister, and niece. The four of us shared a plate of hush puppies and chatted about Rénard's daughter, who is best friends with mine. We swiped through photos of this generation of Southern girls of color, so very much products of the Southern coasts that raised them as well their mothers' itinerance and immigrant heritages. Travel stories are triply at their core.

Like at the start of my trip, I was again plotting a return with my girl to the pristine white sands and full embrace of the Mississippi Gulf. Today, that desire resurfaces. But travel is harder now. There are assistive gadgets to bring, logistic considerations to make. My doctors tell me to set small goals, and to rely on other people for help when I need it. By the time this story goes to print, I'll have outstretched an open hand many times, and received so much care in return.

I'll have, for inspiration, looked up famous brain aneurysm survivors to see what they've achieved. Sharon Stone graced the *Saturday Night Live* stage again. Emilia Clarke went full Targaryen in the series finale of *Game of Thrones.* Joni Mitchell picked up her guitar and kept making music. As for me, I'm here, remembering what coastal Mississippians taught me. I'm here, about to add a period to a sentence. I'm here, writing again.

ACKNOWLEDGMENTS

This is not the book I set out to write when I pitched it to my publisher back in 2019. Neither am I the person I set out to be when this project began, and for these gifts I thank the places I visited between the years 2020 and 2024, and the following people:

Stephen, my love, my best friend, my favorite person, my emergency contact and primary caregiver, whose daily devotion is my well-being, happiness, and healing. I love our life and home, and I'm grateful for all our travels, and I believe I won the cosmic lottery because I get to experience at least one lifetime with you. Your health is my health; your joy is my joy. May we always be the kindest yet most complicated people in the room. May we always be a soft place to land, for each other and for those we come across. In every universe, I love you (more than the cat . . . but don't push your luck).

Anouk, you are the portal through which every good and healing thing enters my life. Thank you for asking for the world—it is a privilege and joy to give it to you. I'd give it to you thrice over if I could. Despite everything that has happened to me and that I've written about, I still believe I am the most fortunate human being to ever walk this earth because you exist and I get to breathe the same air as you. Twin hips, twin hearts, twin journeys. (PS: Do you know where my favorite Madewell sweater is?)

Beocca, the cat whose affection thawed us from the cold, dark days of the pandemic and whose purring and playfulness brought me back to life.

My in-laws in South Carolina, my extended family in New York, and my brother Ali, his wife, and their daughter, who is the jewel of

Manchester—your generosity, care, and caregiving made this book possible and *me* possible again.

Noah, my longtime agent and dearest friend, who shepherds more than just my literary career. I get to tell my little stories because of your big faith in me.

Laura, Carmen, the rest of the Little A crew—how lucky I am to have you all as my team. Your genuine care for me and my family and my work are proof that I signed up for more than just a job. When I became a Little A author, I was really becoming part of a friendship pact with one mission: make something beautiful out of my truth. I am so grateful that you always meet my attention and devotion with yours, and for your trust and patience that carry me through long days and even longer years of writing.

Chris, Christen, James, Linda, Meghan, Becca, Sandy, Angel, Jamison, Kelly, Maureen, Melissa, my cousins Jen and Vam, Erin, Stephanie, Buki and Kyle, Nancy and Jesse, and Jill from afar—you all stood on the front lines of my recovery battle. You were my hands and feet when I could barely move, my voice when I didn't have the words, my light when it was too painful to shine my own. Of course, you were and are my heart. What am I but the kindness you give me? I am so rich, and my life is so full because I have each of you.

Stephen's colleagues (particularly the middle school team), Anouk's friends and teammates (and their families), our Lenevar neighbors—you caught us with your love.

Friends, friends of friends, acquaintances, readers and Bookstagrammers everywhere—I don't know why you're so good to me. Your gifts, homemade meals, and GoFundMe donations afforded me time to heal, get stronger, and finish this book.

My writing community, which stretches far beyond Charleston. From my Converse MFA family and Sackett Street classes to the Kweli, VONA, Kundiman, Catapult, Lighthouse, Writing Workshops Dallas, Hub City, and Pulitzer communities—you spoil me with your love, support, and kindness, especially Jennie, Kerri, Cameron, Minda, Cielo, Krysten, Ebba, Mark, Olivia, and Deb.

To every person who sent or dropped off meals when I couldn't cook for myself and my family, thank you, and I hope to one day have you over for the biggest dinner party ever.

To Vivian, my North Star in publishing and in life. I love and adore you, and our correspondences during my recovery year kept me writing.

To Ceara, for always knowing what to say, when, how little or much, and whose pursuit of dreams and motherhood greatly inspire and fortify mine. May we never stray from who we truly are.

To my friends Anya and Connie and Luca—friends first, neuroscientist and medical professionals second. You were put on this earth to help us all heal and understand the messes that are our lives. Charleston is kinder, healthier, happier, smarter, truer with you in it.

To Dani and Rafa, after whom we model our travels and with whom we share our love of street foods and fine dining.

To my medical team: Dr. Blue at the emergency room at Roper Saint Francis, the EMTs who ambulated me to MUSC, Drs. Lena, Hubbard, Porto, et al. Thank you for saving my life.

To my nurses, nurse techs, neuro PTs, speech language pathologist, neuropsychologist, ophthalmologist, neuro ophthalmologist, neuro caregiver support group, and the Brain Injury Association of South Carolina. Thank you for saving my living.

To the patient, supportive team at *Travel + Leisure*, especially my editor Liz. Thank you for letting me include the longer version of my travel essay as an epilogue to this book. (The original appears in the February 2025 "Water" issue of the magazine.) The publishing world, and the world in general, is more humane *and* more human with you in it.

Big thanks to *Coastal Living* magazine and editor Tracey Minkin, who gave me my first glossy travel magazine assignment, which appears here in an edited version ("Casual Crabbing"). You kicked open a door—how dare you believe in me! Meeting you gave me a new confidence in my prose.

All my admiration for and gratitude to early readers and faithful cheerleaders Grace M. Cho, M. Evelina Galang, Megha Majumdar, Aimee Nezhukumatathil, Grace Talusan, Matt Ortile, Annabelle Tometich, and Nicole Chung.

To the baking team at Harbinger Cafe and the baristas at Starbucks on Sam Rittenberg Boulevard, thank you for providing me with cozy places to write.

To my daughter's volleyball coaches and her teammates (and their families): You fostered her development in sports and supported her and gave her a joyful place to be during a difficult time. Never underestimate the power of distraction: Extracurriculars bring us back from the depths and to ourselves. And as well, Anouk's wise words apply to you: *We have a good team.*

This book would not be here if it weren't for the financial support and esteem of the Sustainable Arts Foundation, AIR Serenbe and Capita, Pasadena Literary Alliance, the South Carolina Commission for Minority Affairs, and the Authors League Fund.

To Kylie Minogue, with whom I share a birthday. To Sharon Stone, Emilia Clarke, Joni Mitchell, and Dr. Dre, my fellow brain aneurysm survivors who didn't give up on their art. To Maggie Rogers, whose music wakes me up every morning and keeps me just sad enough so I can get into the "truthiness" of my writing. To Anthony Bourdain, whose television shows and writing allowed me to be an armchair traveler when I didn't yet have a valid passport or the financial means to see the world.

To the people of Cebu, my heart is with you as you recover and rebuild after the earthquakes and typhoons. May environmental justice prevail.

Last but not the least, I'd like to thank myself for staying here, for coming back to the page, for holding on and letting go, and for always going against the odds. May you continue to fight entropy, defy the norm, and live deep into the person you were meant to be. You did it, and you'll do it again, inspiring hope in a way that's truly yours and yours alone.

To help save Palawan's natural beauty and endemic wildlife, please visit https://centreforsustainabilityph.org.

ABOUT THE AUTHOR

Photo © 2025 Buki Peters

Cinelle Barnes is the author of *Monsoon Mansion: A Memoir* and *Malaya: Essays on Freedom*. She is also the editor of *A Measure of Belonging: Twenty-One Writers of Color on the New American South*. Cinelle is a brain aneurysm survivor and sits on the Brain Injury Leadership Council of South Carolina. Books have been the one constant in her life—through her tumultuous childhood in the Philippines, her years living as an undocumented immigrant in New York City, her time as a new bride living in the American South, and as she completed her MFA program and began writing about her truths. She lives in Charleston with her husband, daughter, and cat. For more information, visit cinellebarnes.com and follow her on Instagram @cinellebarnesbooks.